The Purrfect Book
of
Cat Cartoons

Featuring Cartoons From
Barron's
The New Yorker
The Wall Street Journals
and more!

Front Cover illustration: Charlie Hankin

Introduction: Bob Mankoff
Book Design: Darren Kornblut

Dedicated to Jennifer & Bea

Cartoon Collections, LLC
10 Grand Central, 29th Floor
New York, NY 10017

For cartoon licensing information visit www.cartoonstock.com
Create a personalized version of this book at www.cartoonstockgifts.com

First edition published 2022

ISBN: 978-1-963079-03-6 / Item # 46496

Introduction

Bob Mankoff, former Cartoon Editor of *The New Yorker* magazine, here. For over twenty years as Cartoon editor, I poured over thousands of submissions each week, critiquing, editing, and helping select those that would go in the magazine.

You might be surprised to know that that was not always a laugh fest. First, even the best cartoonists produce their fair share of clunkers, just like even the best baseball players often strike out–especially if they're on my team.

One kind of cartoon, however, could always lighten the mood. A good cat cartoon! When one of those came across my desk, I would get very excited and pat it and smooch it, saying, "Who's a good little kitty cartoon?", "Who's a good kitty cat toon?" "You are! You are!" And what you've got here awaiting you as you turn these pages is even better. So much better. A whole book of very good kitty cat cartoons from *The New Yorker, The Wall Street Journal, Barron's*, and *The American Bystander*.

As a cat owner and lover, I really relate to these cartoons, and you will too. I guarantee it! 100%! And if that doesn't work for you, 75%! Really, these cartoons are as loveable and relatable as the smoochy kittens we adore, some with classic cat monikers like Buttons, Smokey, Sheeba, Neela and Kitty, as well as more unusual ones like Pickles, Furball, and Keyboard. Actually, I made that last one up, but I bet someone has named their cat Keyboard.

I hope you enjoy these cartoons while curled up with your little (or big) furbaby and have a laugh together.

MAINFRAME

LAPTOP

POCKET

1

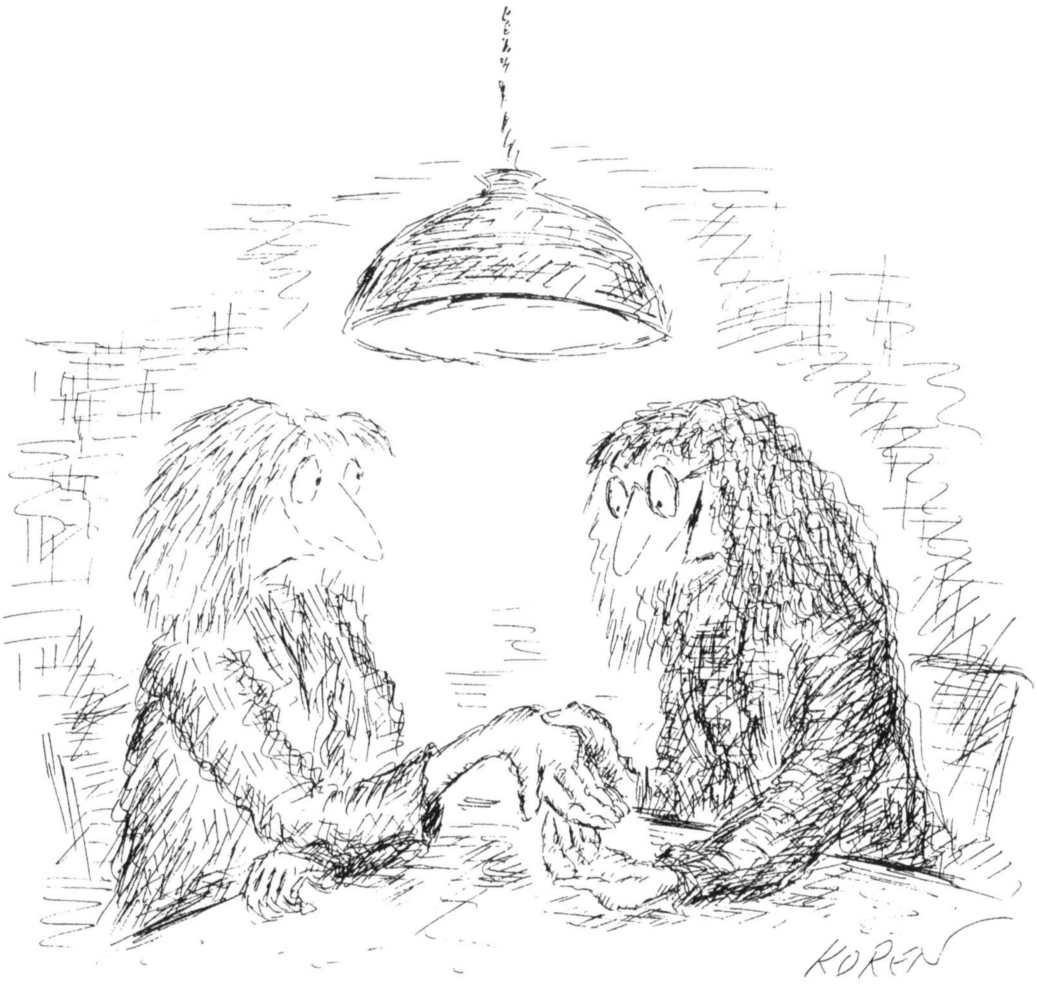
KOREN

"A wonderful cat is coming into your life."

"...and how much experience have you of sushi making?"

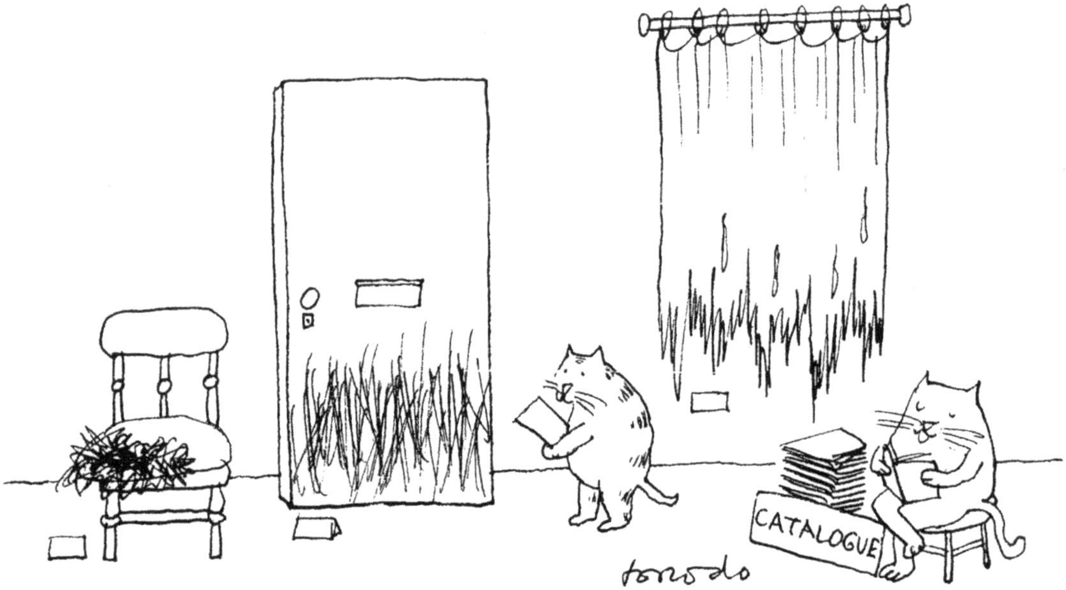
CATALOGUE

ALLOW ME.
Hankin

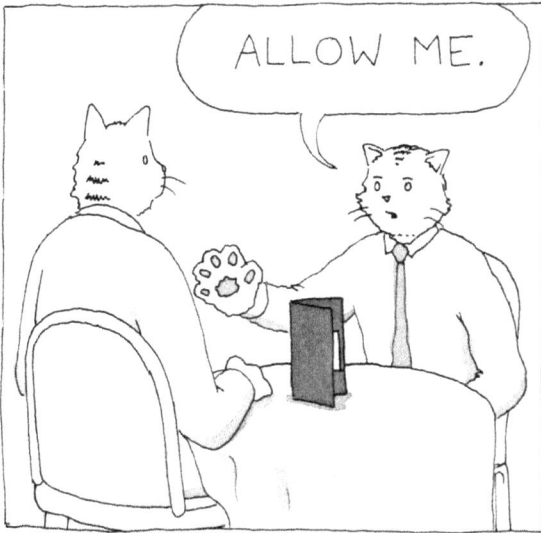

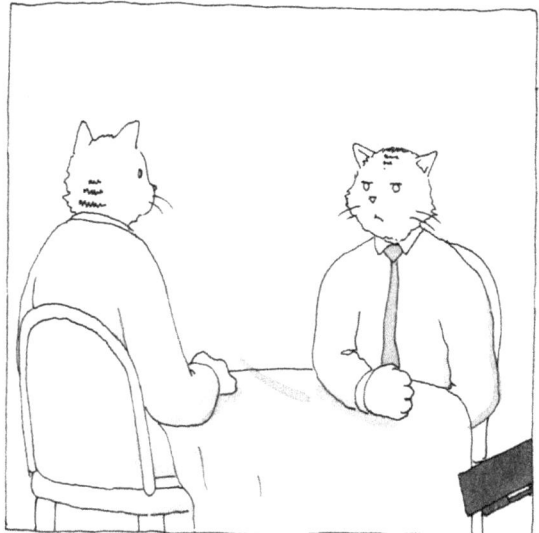

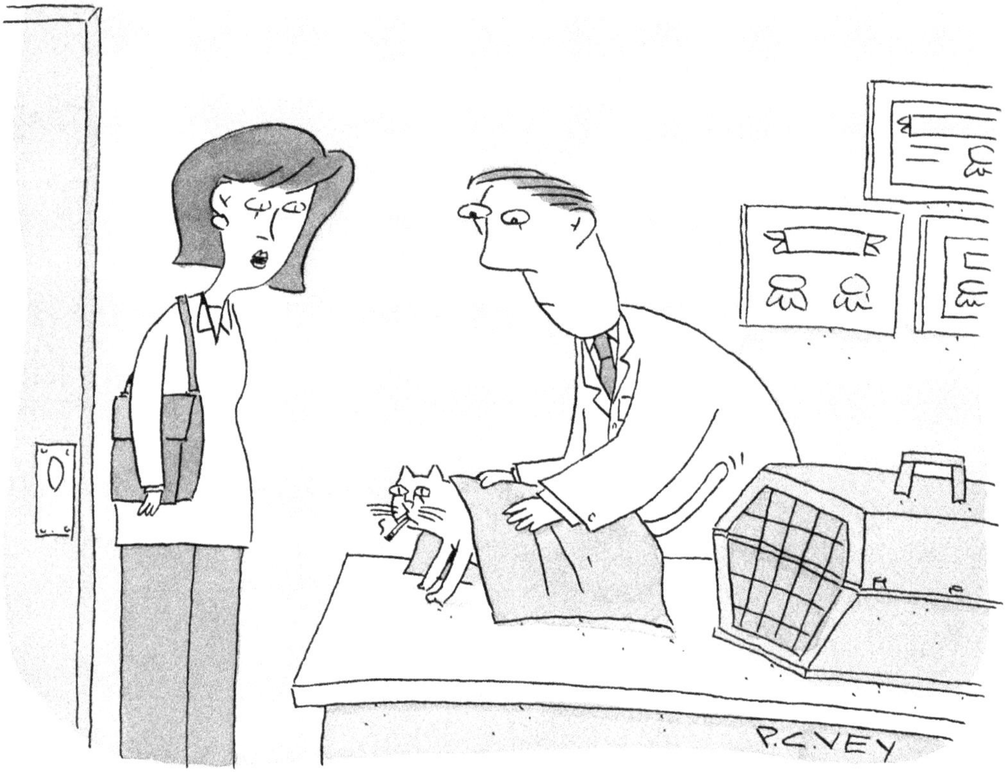
P.C.VEY

"He's so old I usually let him do what he wants."

"It's curiosity and your HMO won't cover it."

"I'm tired of just scratching out a living."

"*You make me want to be a better mouser.*"

"No, I haven't confronted him. I guess I'm a pussycat."

"*You make me want to be a better mouser.*"

"No, I haven't confronted him. I guess I'm a pussycat."

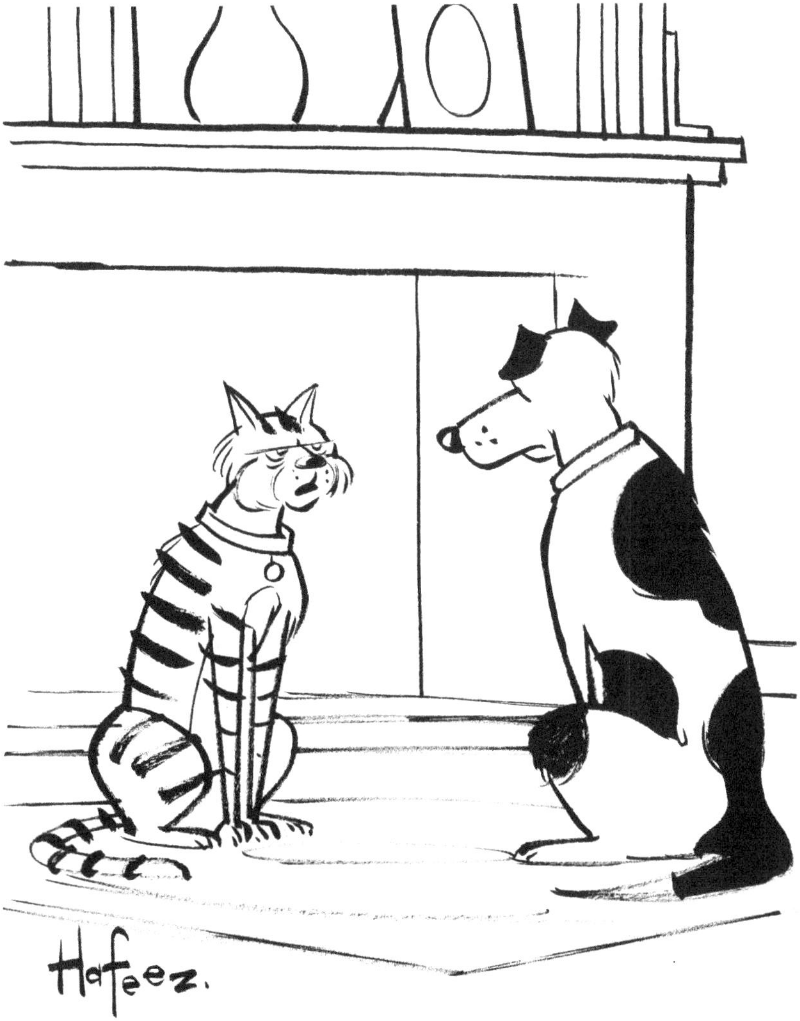
Hafeez.

"If I don't get a good twenty-three hours, I'm a wreck."

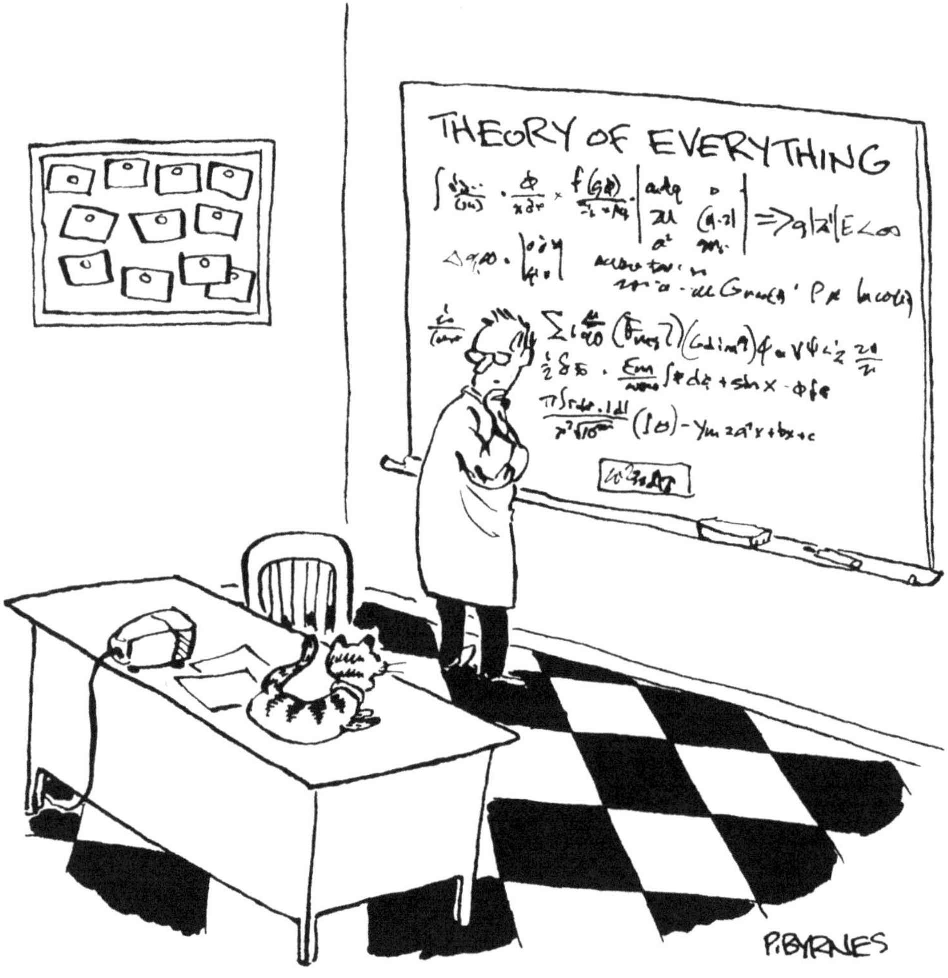
THEORY OF EVERYTHING
P.BYRNES

"Still doesn't explain cats."

"I'm listening – I just need to chase this insect real quick."

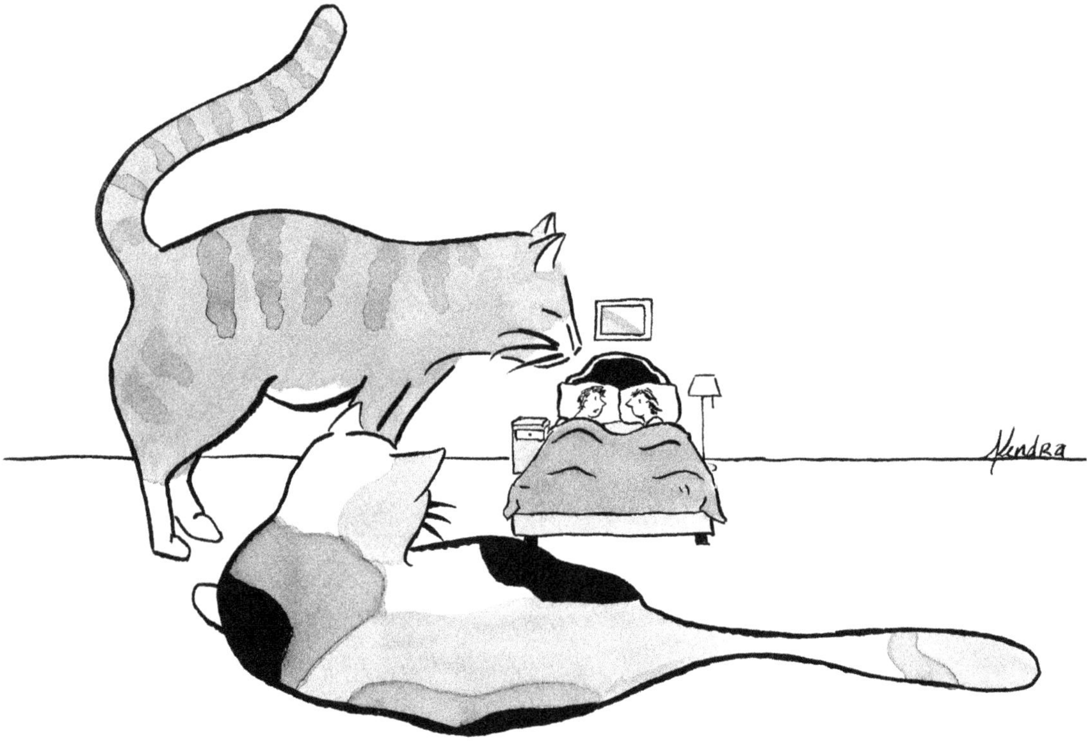
Kendra

"It's not that I don't 'like' your cats."

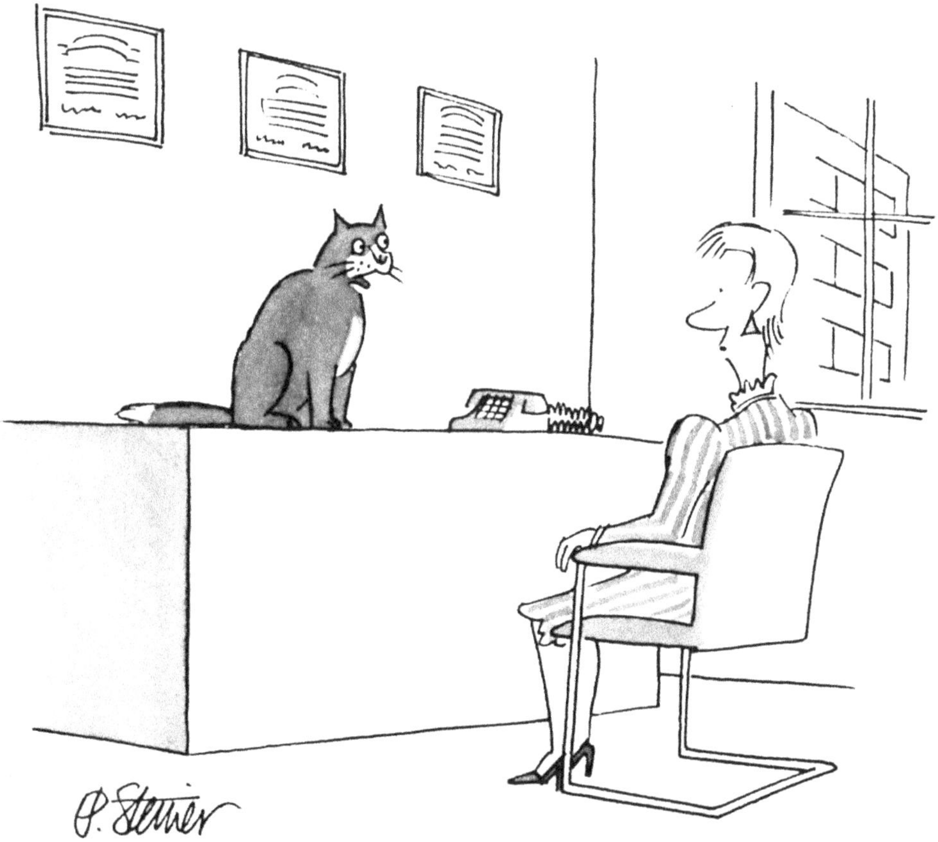
P. Steiner

"I'd like you to have a CAT scan."

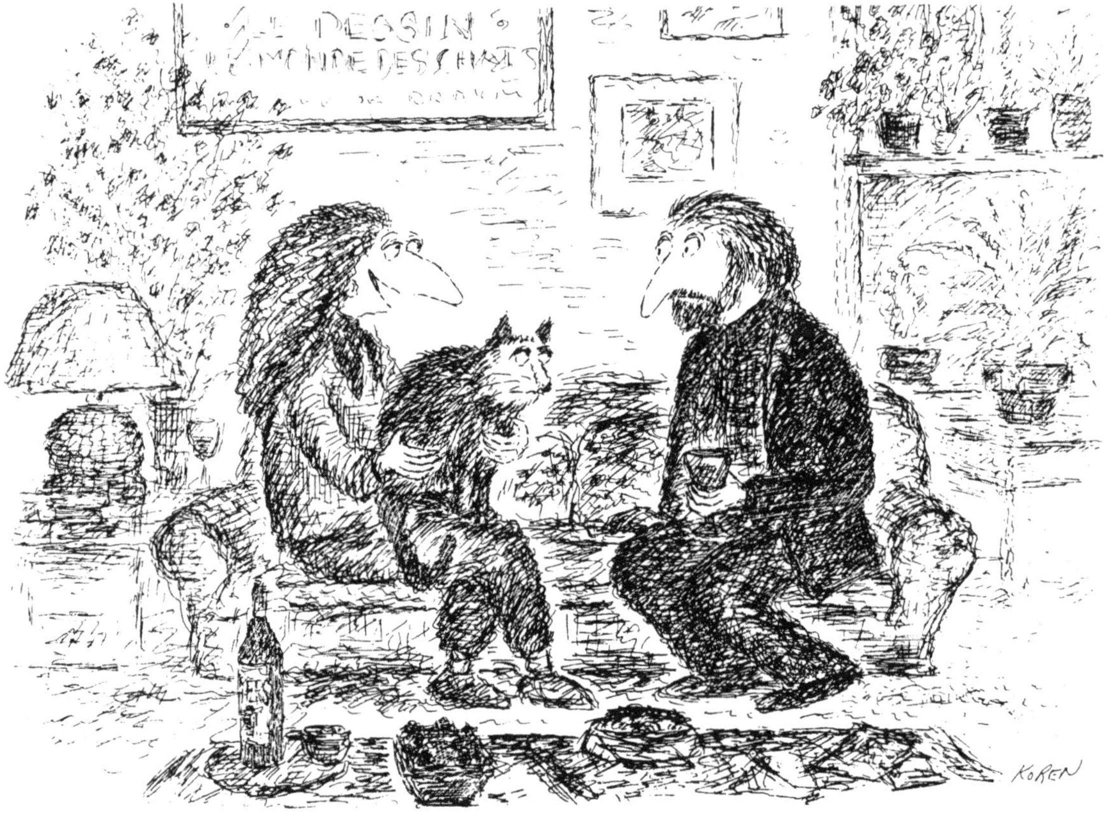
KOREN

"Around here his word is law."

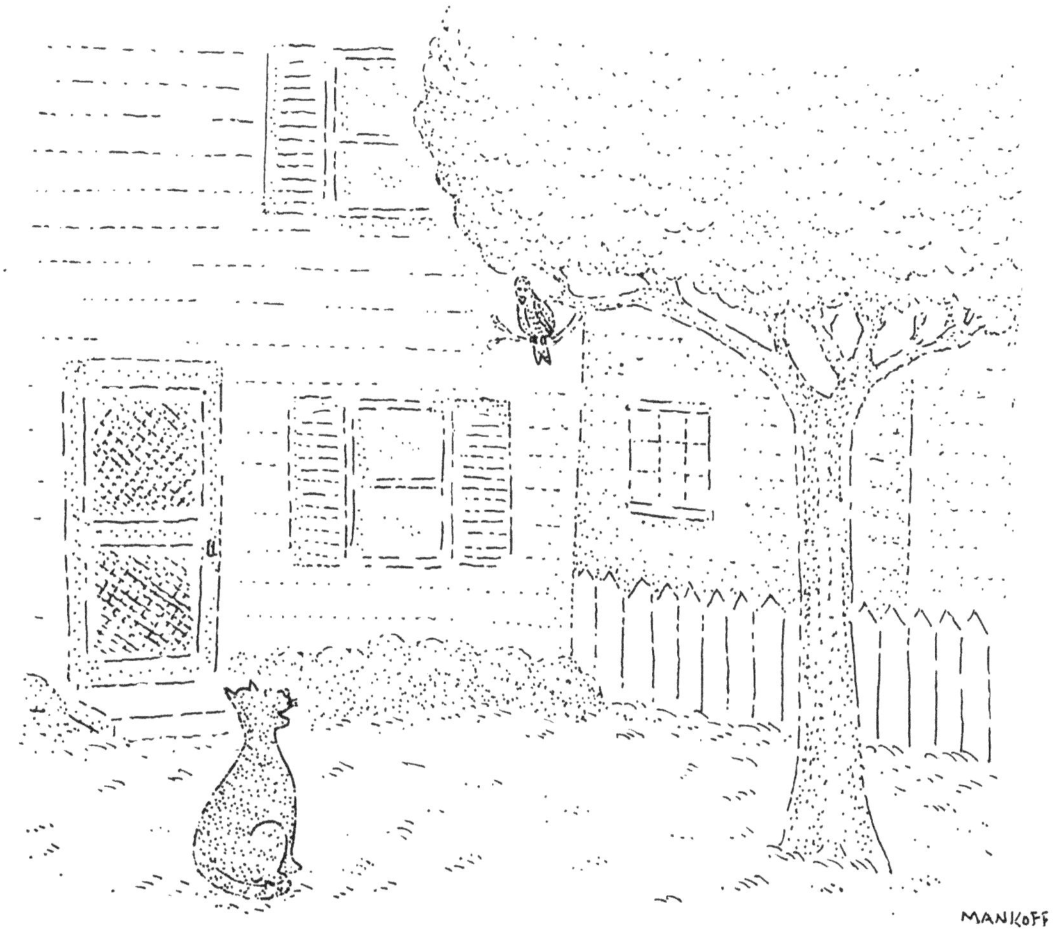
MANKOFF

"Hey, let's do lunch."

"*I stay inside until I'm positive I'm not on the menu anywhere near by.*"

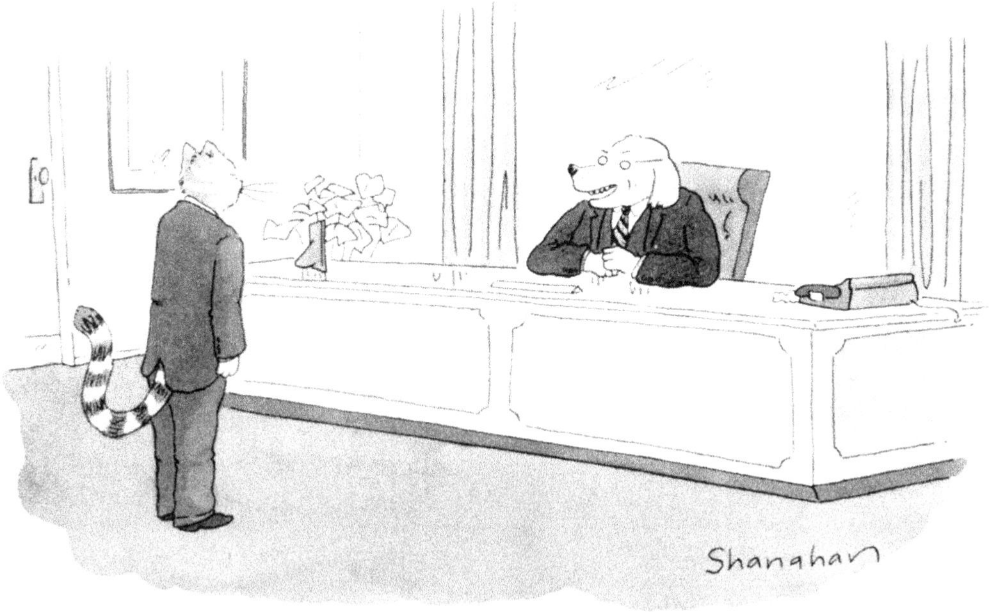
Shanahan

"I'm not worried about you. You'll land on your feet."

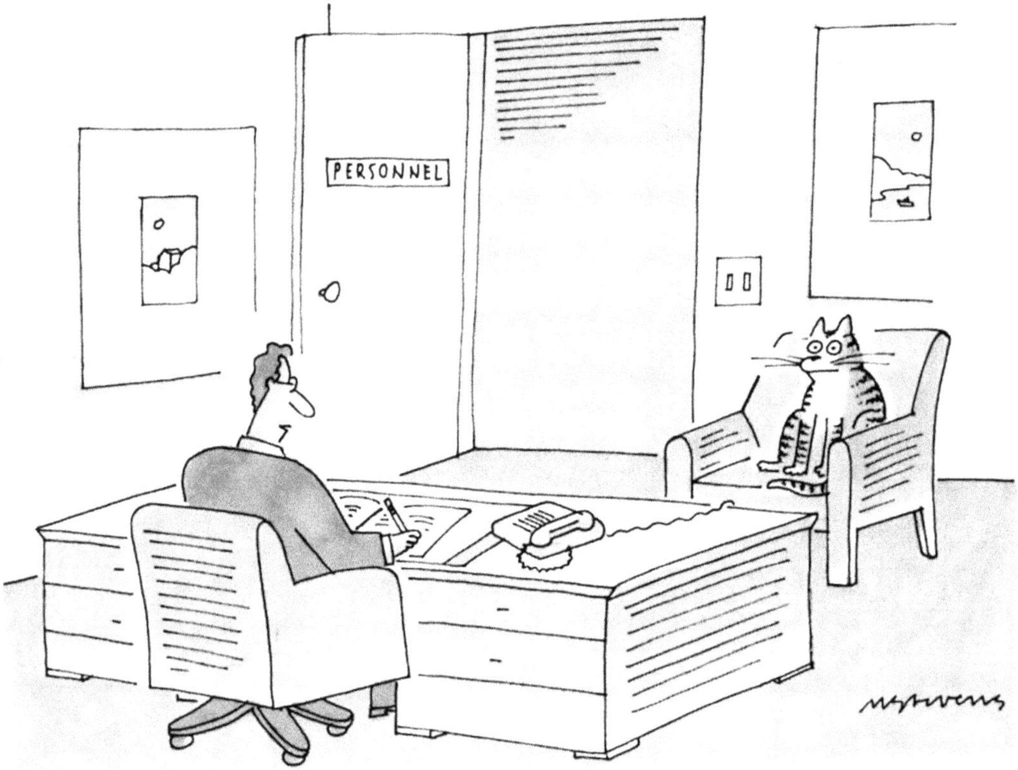
PERSONNEL

"And where have you previously moused?"

"I've been wondering if there isn't some way _we_ could capitalize on the cat craze."

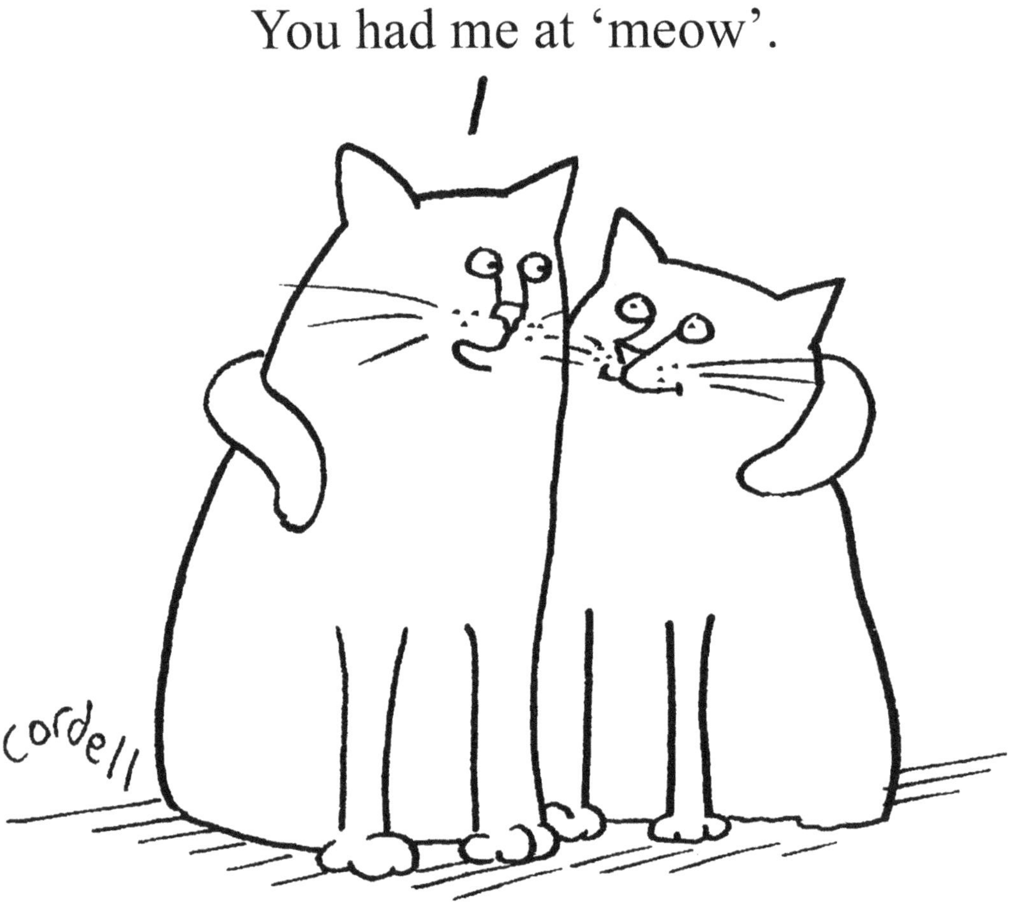
You had me at 'meow'.
cordell

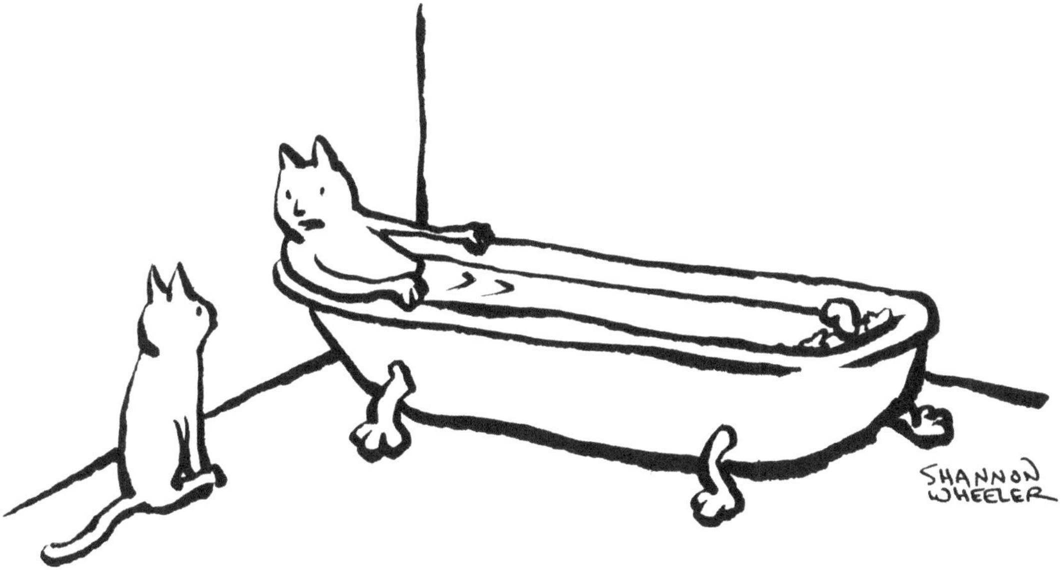
SHANNON
WHEELER

*"Lick. Lick. Lick. Lick. Lick. Lick. Lick. Lick. Lick.
Lick. Lick. Lick. Lick. Lick. Lick. Lick. Lick. Lick.
Then I thought, why not just take a real bath."*

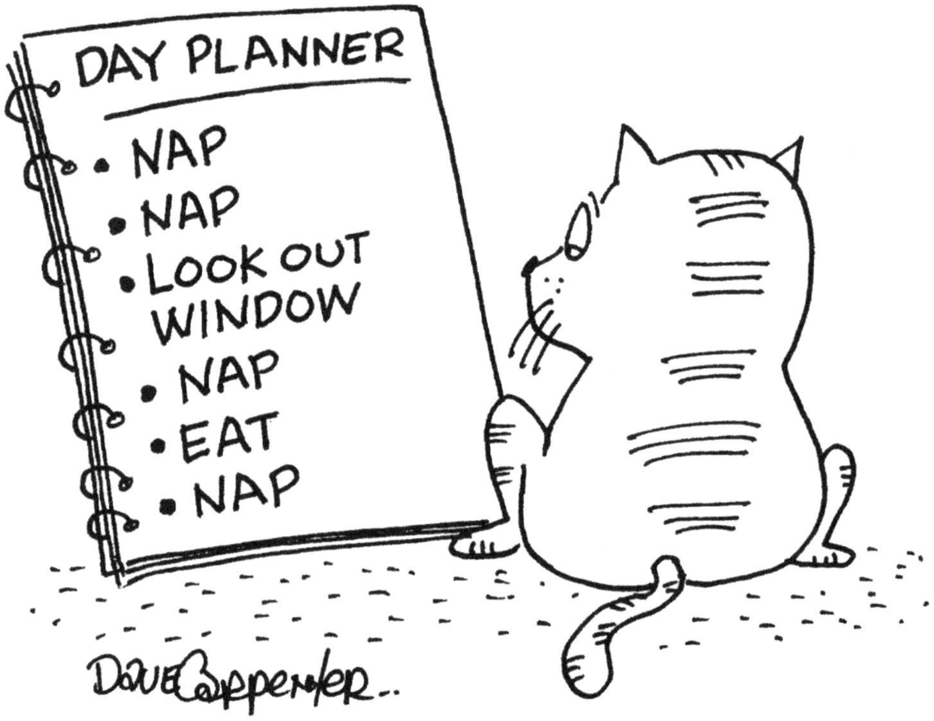
DAY PLANNER
• NAP
• NAP
• LOOK OUT WINDOW
• NAP
• EAT
• NAP

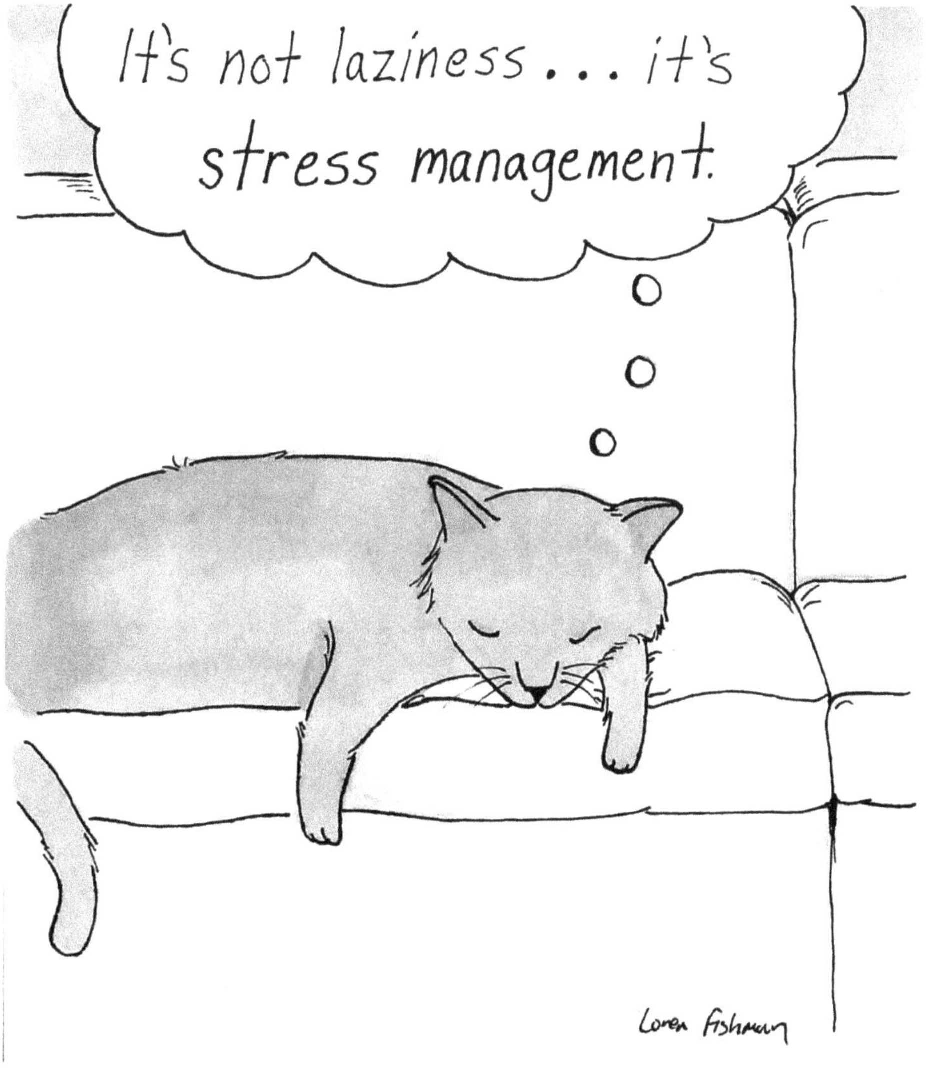
It's not laziness . . . it's stress management.
Loren Fishman

"If you must know, Jimmy, you came from a box in front of the market. It said 'Free Kittens.'"

Senior Cat
Warranty
* Low maintenance
sofa accessory
* Unlimited purring
and cuddling
* Mellow "been there,
done that"
attitude

jjhubal

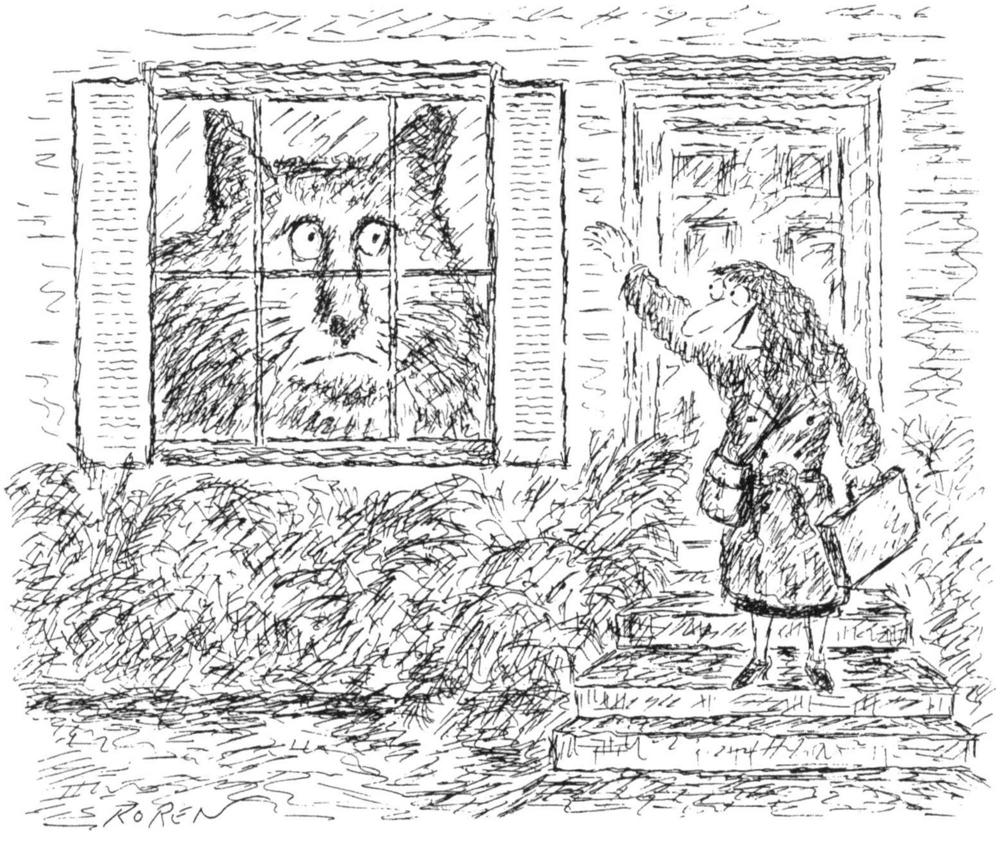
S ROREN

"Love you!"

"You fed me tuna and cleaned my litter box, Harris, and I'm not going to forget it."

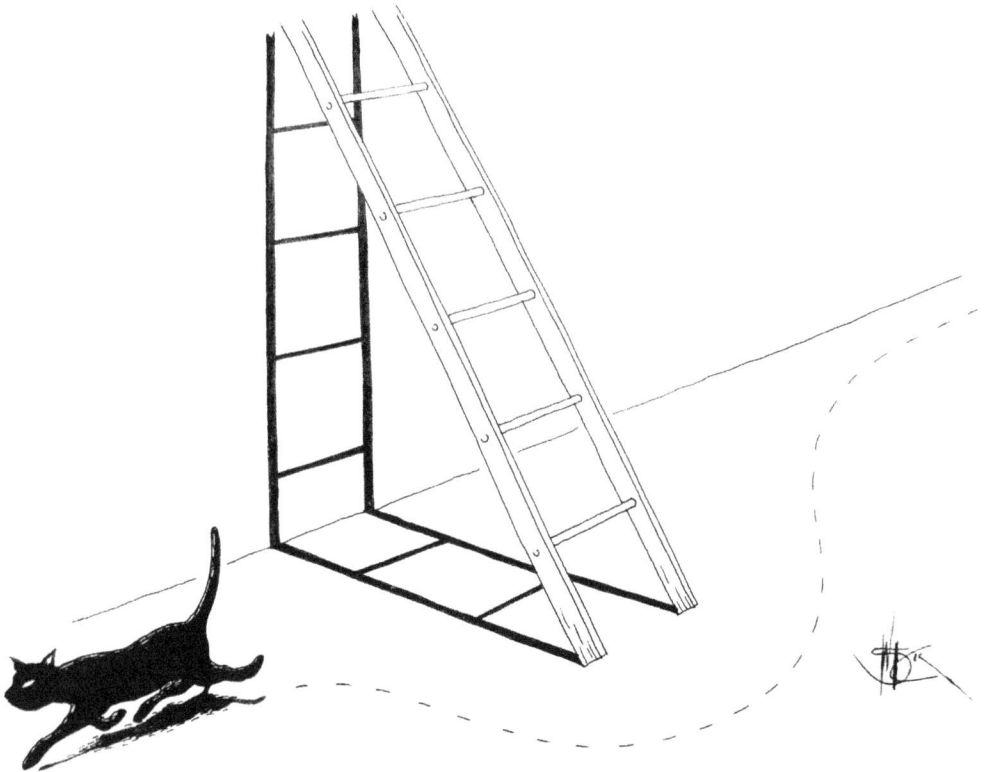

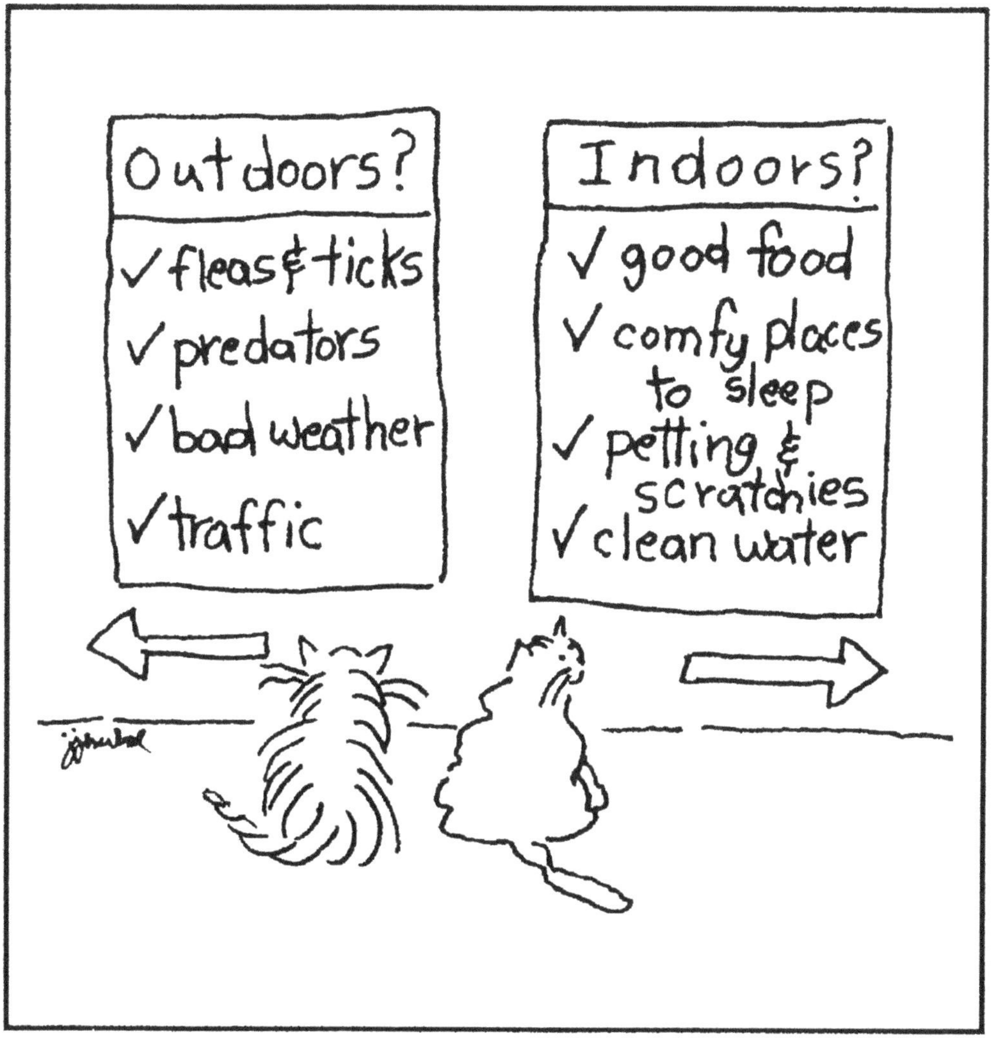
Outdoors?
✓fleas & ticks
✓predators
✓bad weather
✓traffic
Indoors?
✓good food
✓comfy places to sleep
✓petting & scratchies
✓clean water

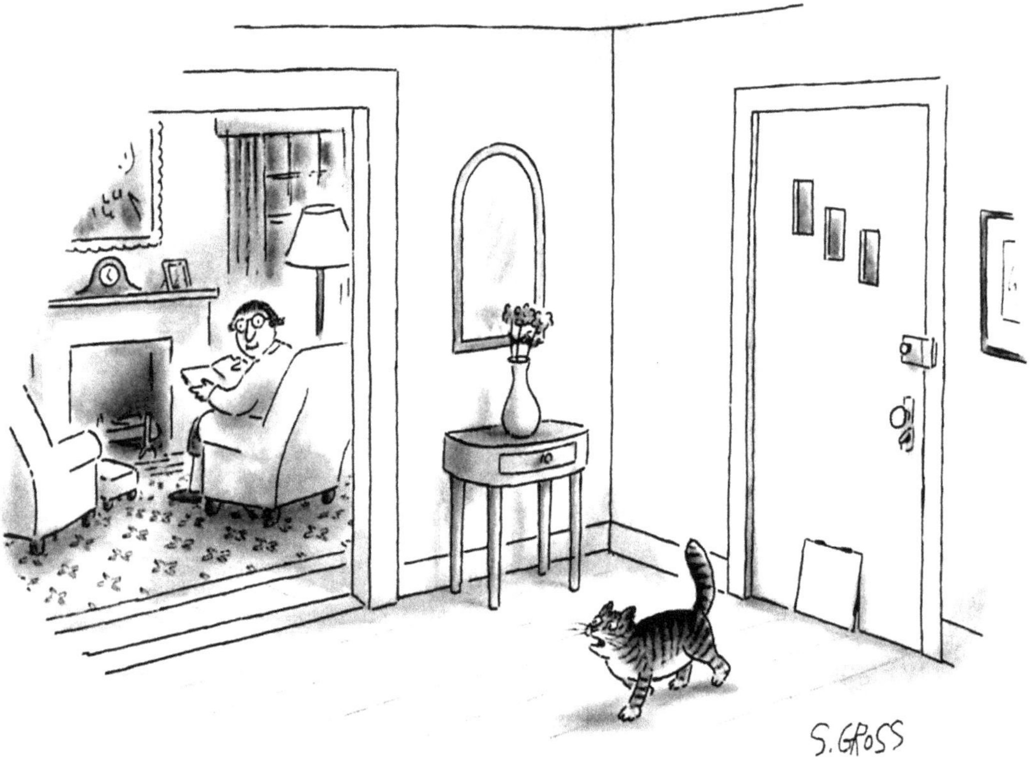
S. GROSS

"Honey, I'm home!"

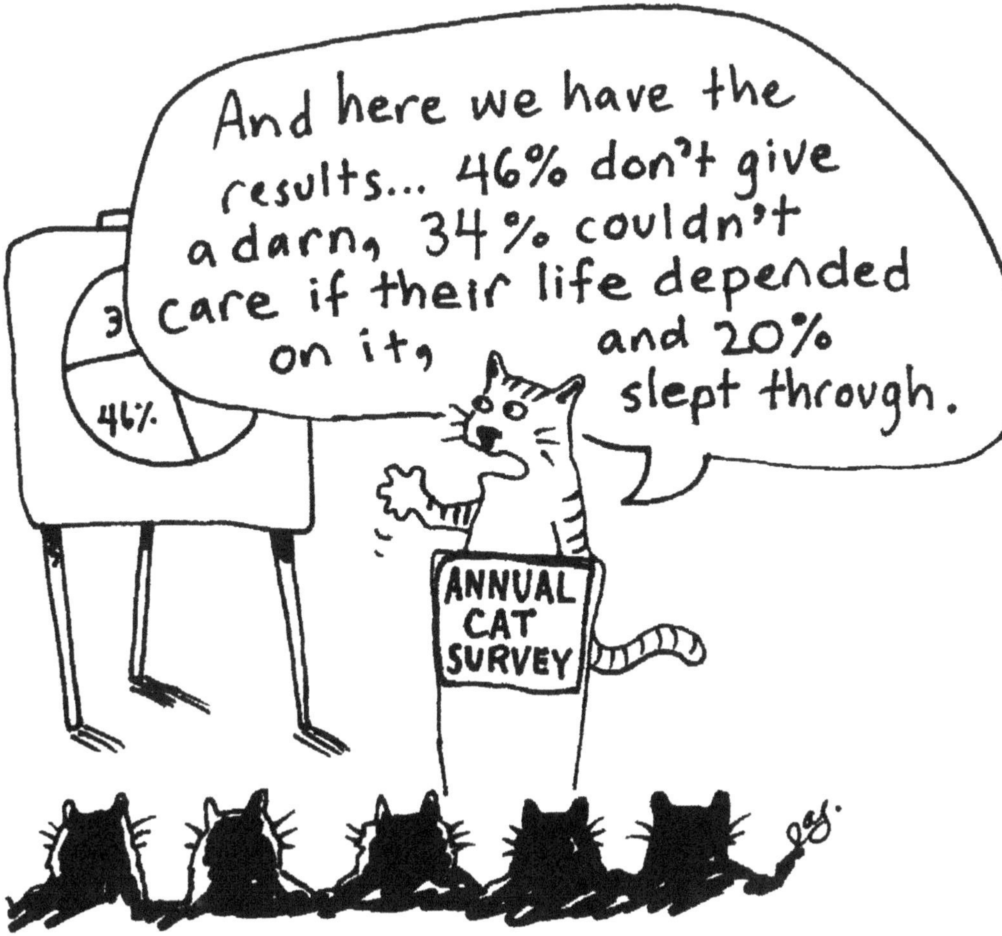
And here we have the results... 46% don't give a darn, 34% couldn't care if their life depended on it, and 20% slept through.
ANNUAL CAT SURVEY
46%

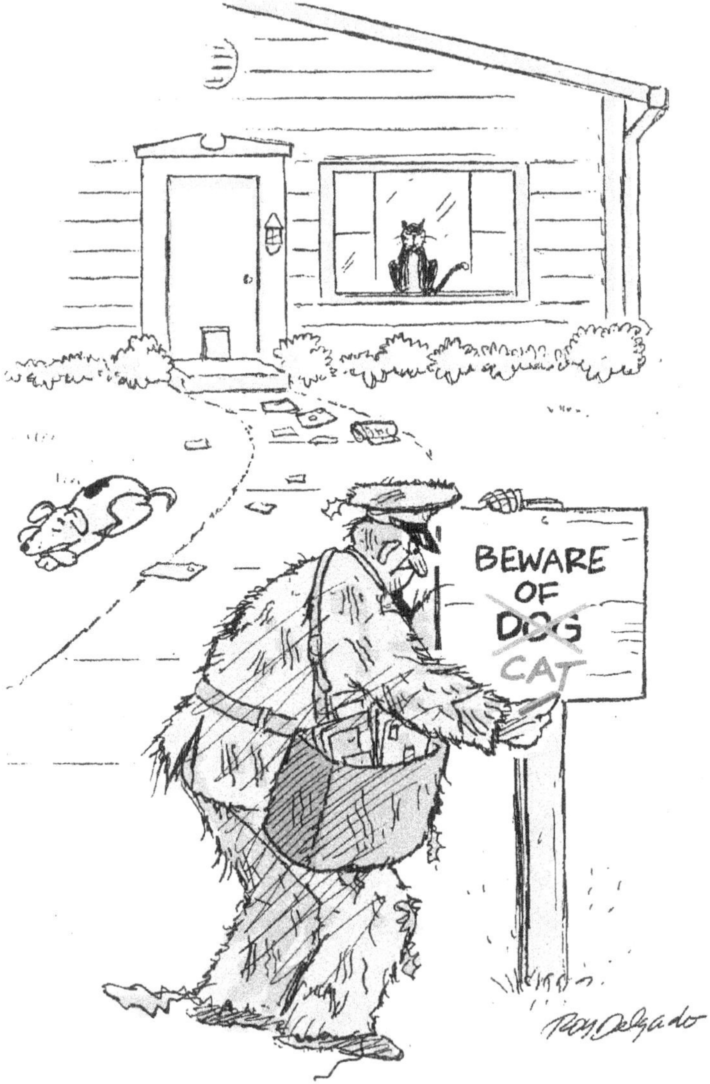
BEWARE
OF
DOG
CAT
Roy Delgado

"Then one day he said, 'It's either me or the damned cat!'"

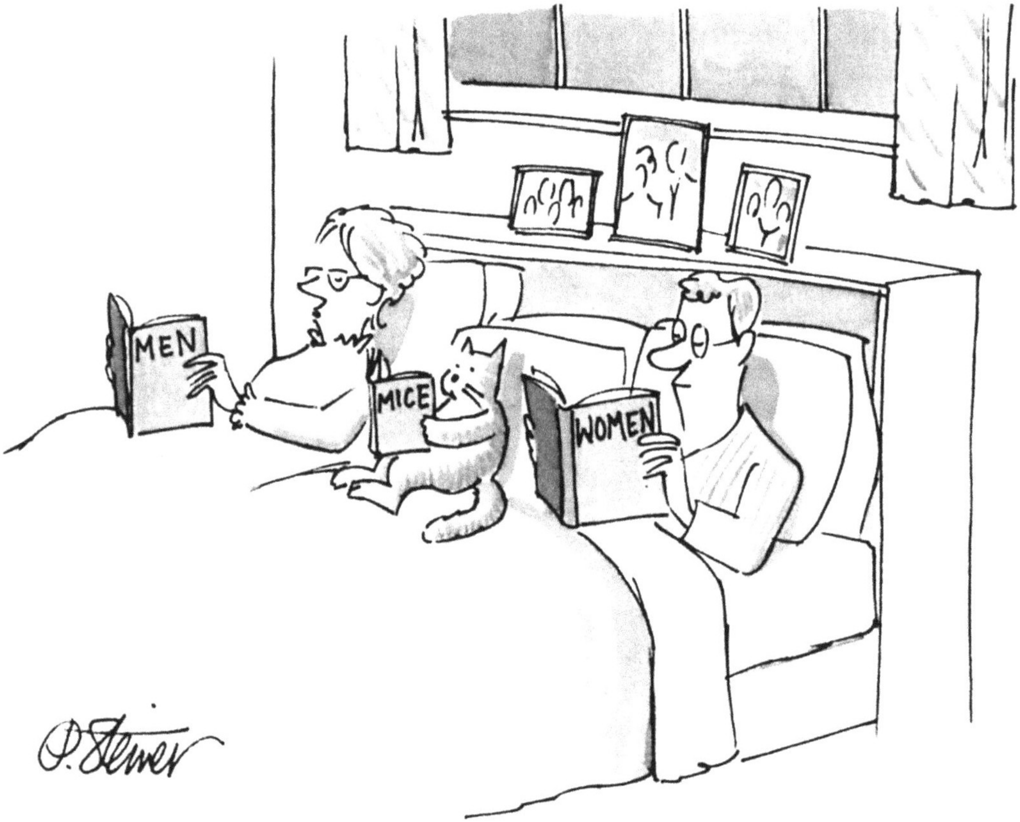
MEN
MICE
WOMEN
P. Steiner

THE AMAZING ADVENTURES OF
WONDERCAT
ZISSER

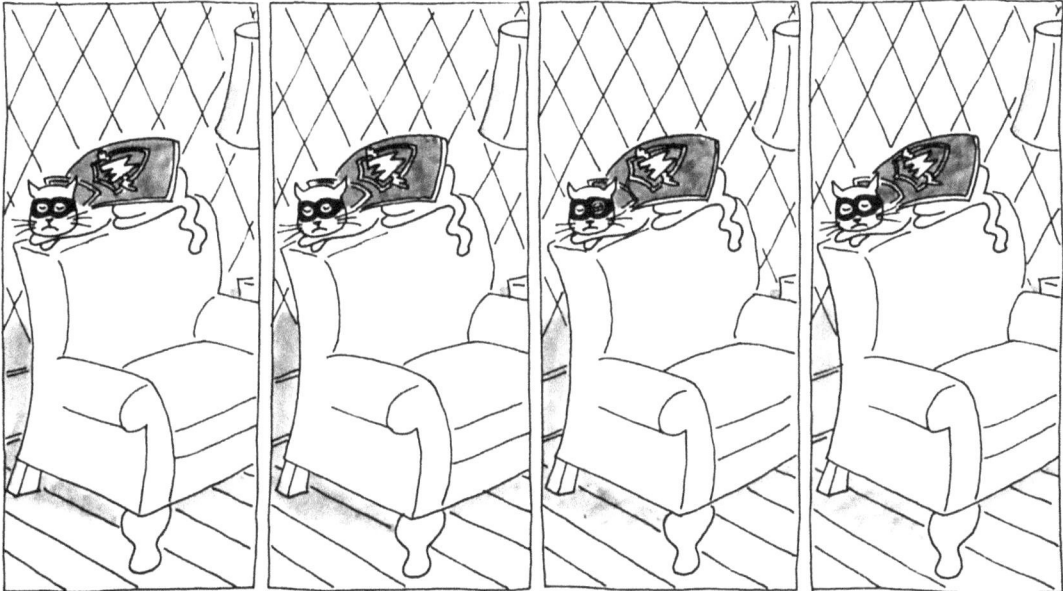

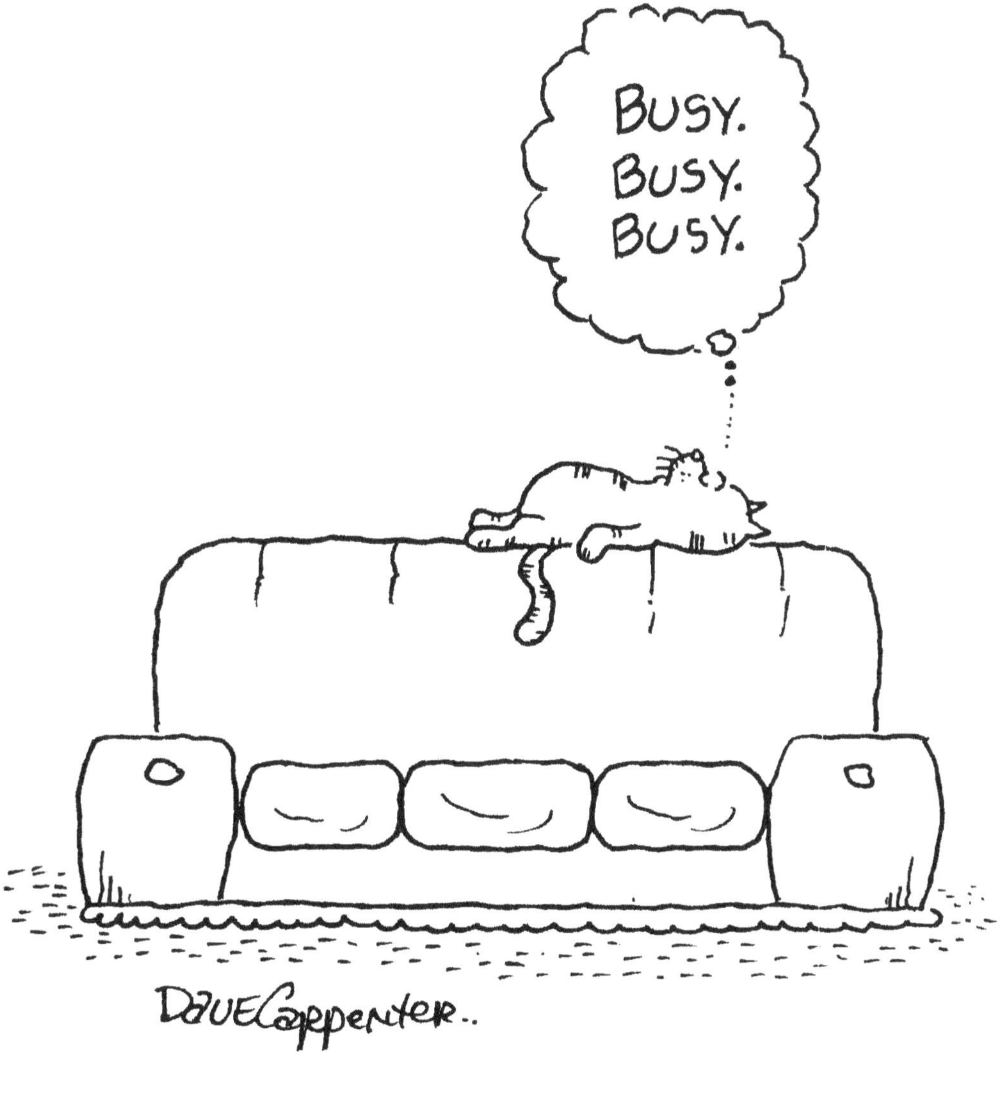
BUSY.
BUSY.
BUSY.
DAVE CARPENTER..

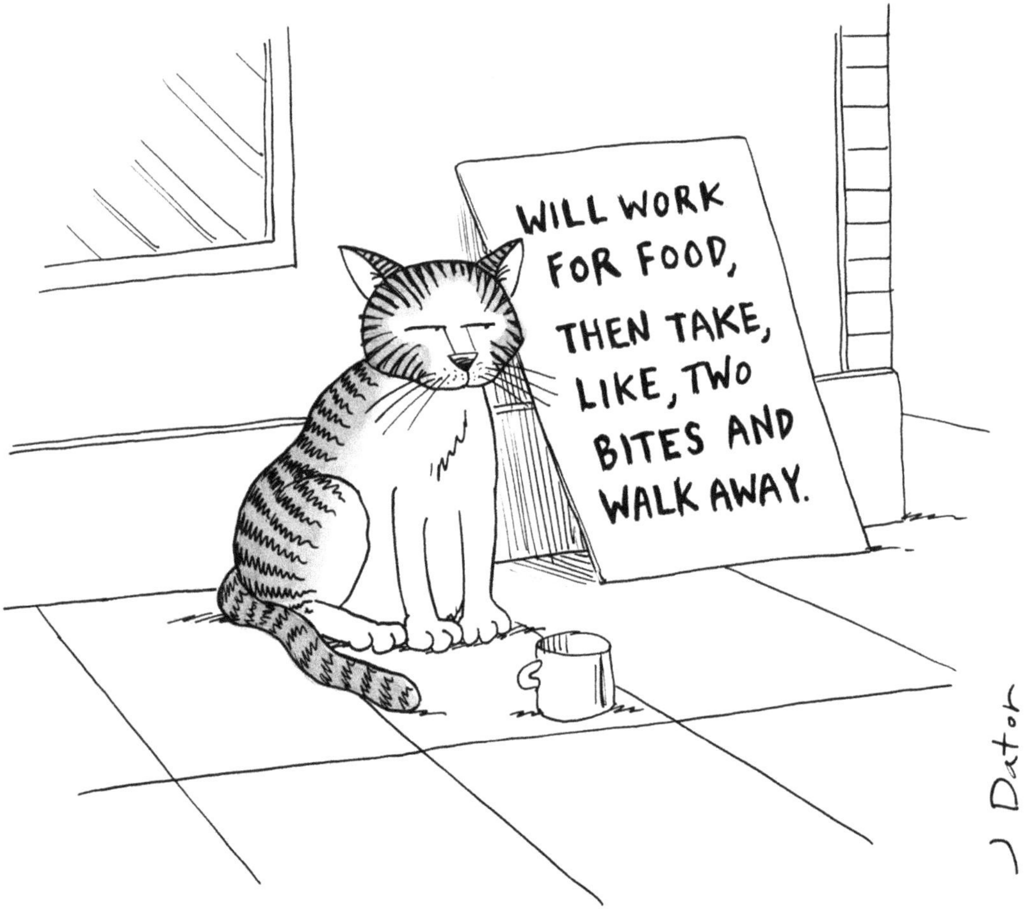
WILL WORK FOR FOOD, THEN TAKE, LIKE, TWO BITES AND WALK AWAY.
J Dator

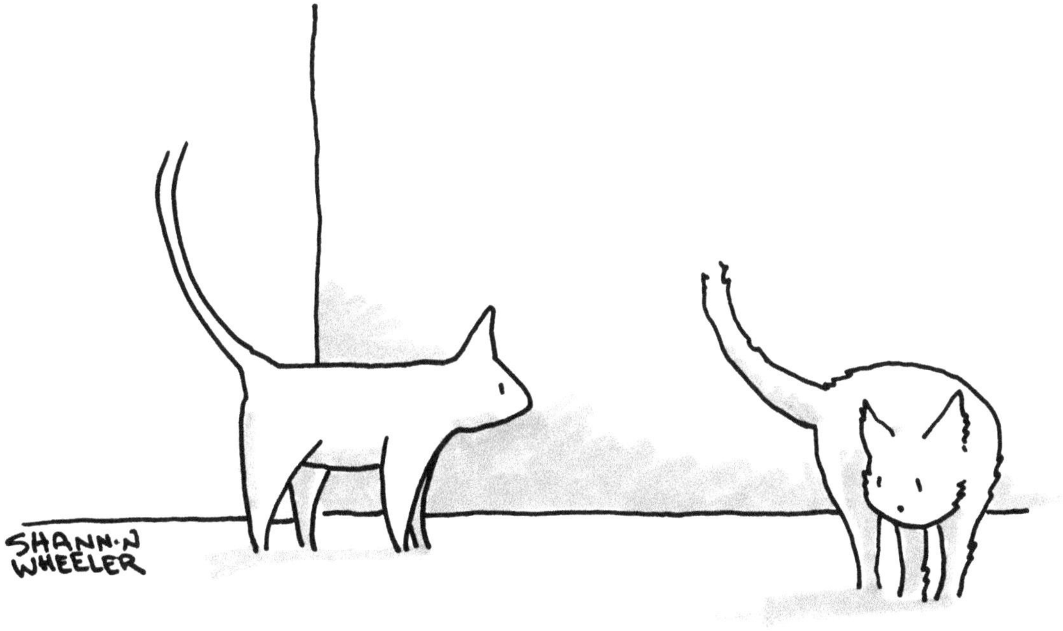
SHANNON
WHEELER

"Didn't I see you on YouTube riding a Roomba?"

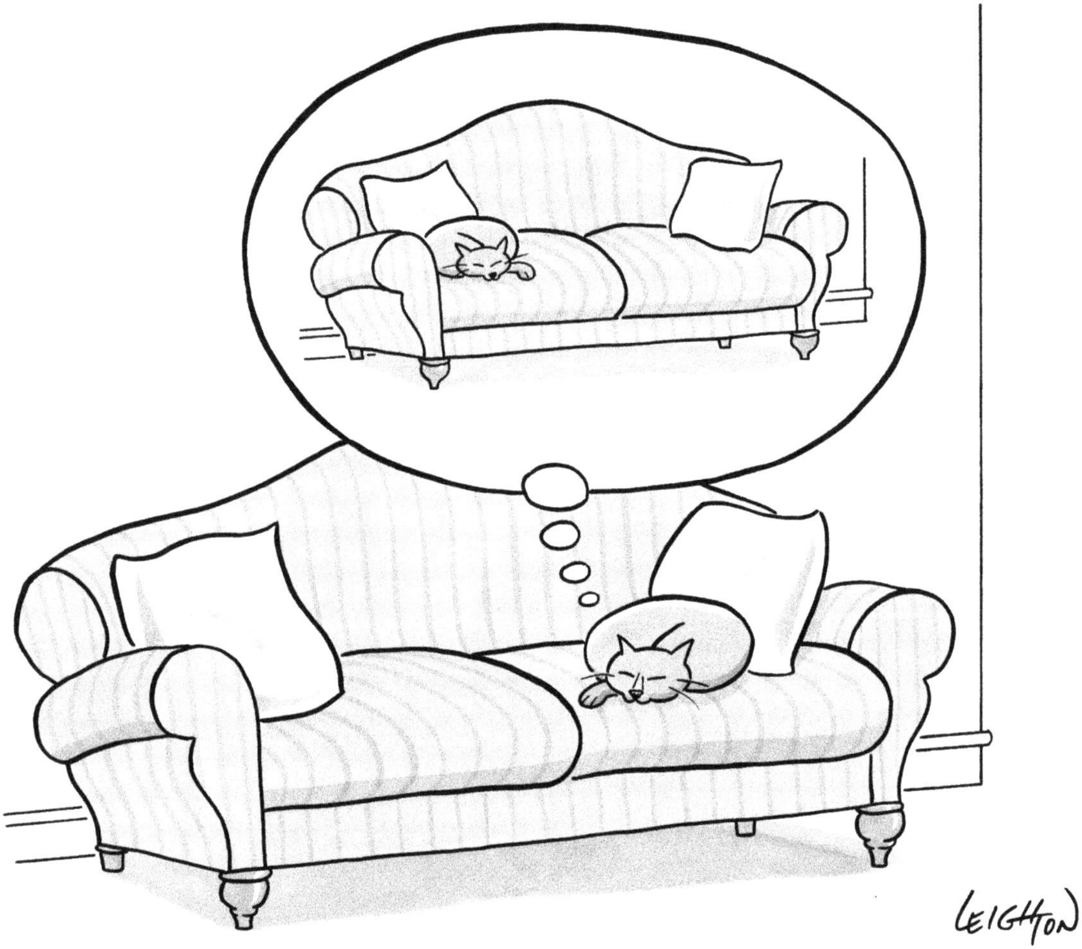
LEIGHTON

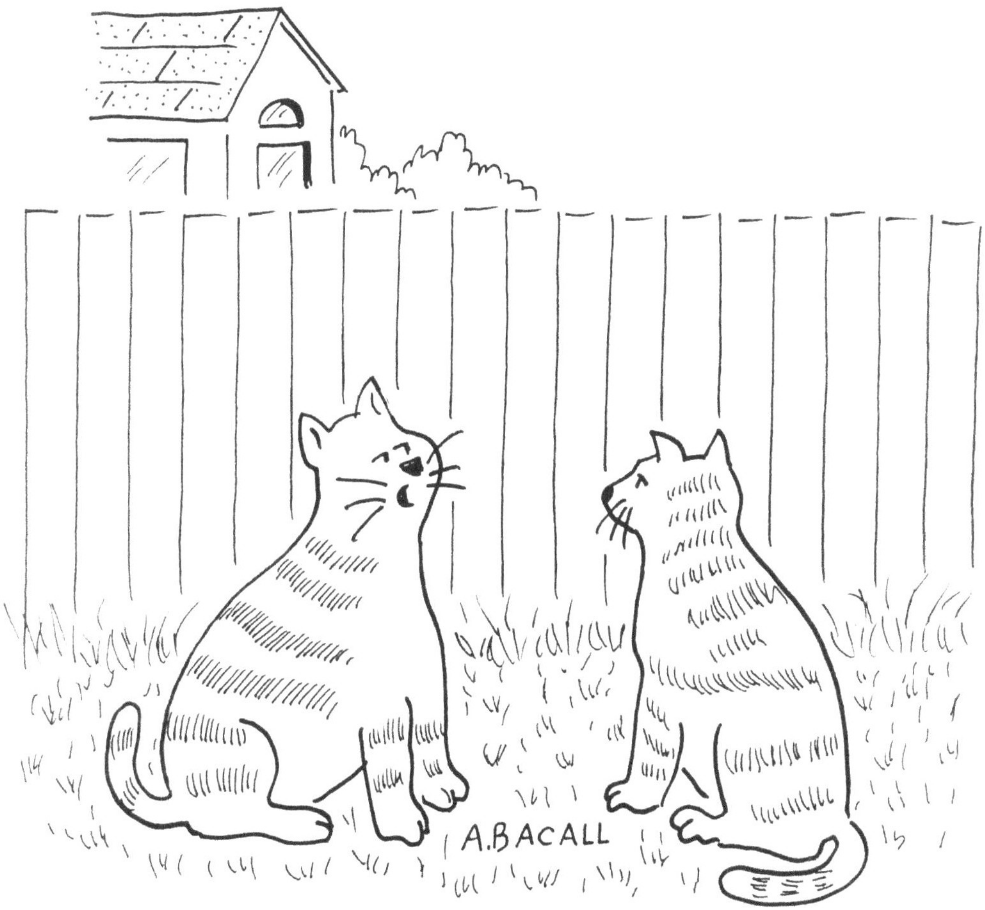
A.BACALL

"I take lots of antioxidants. That's why I'm still on the first of my nine lives."

"If it weren't for you, I would have conquered the world by now."

"*Isn't it true that you did not love the victim, as you claim, but, in point of fact, feigned affection for the sole purpose of obtaining tuna fish?*"

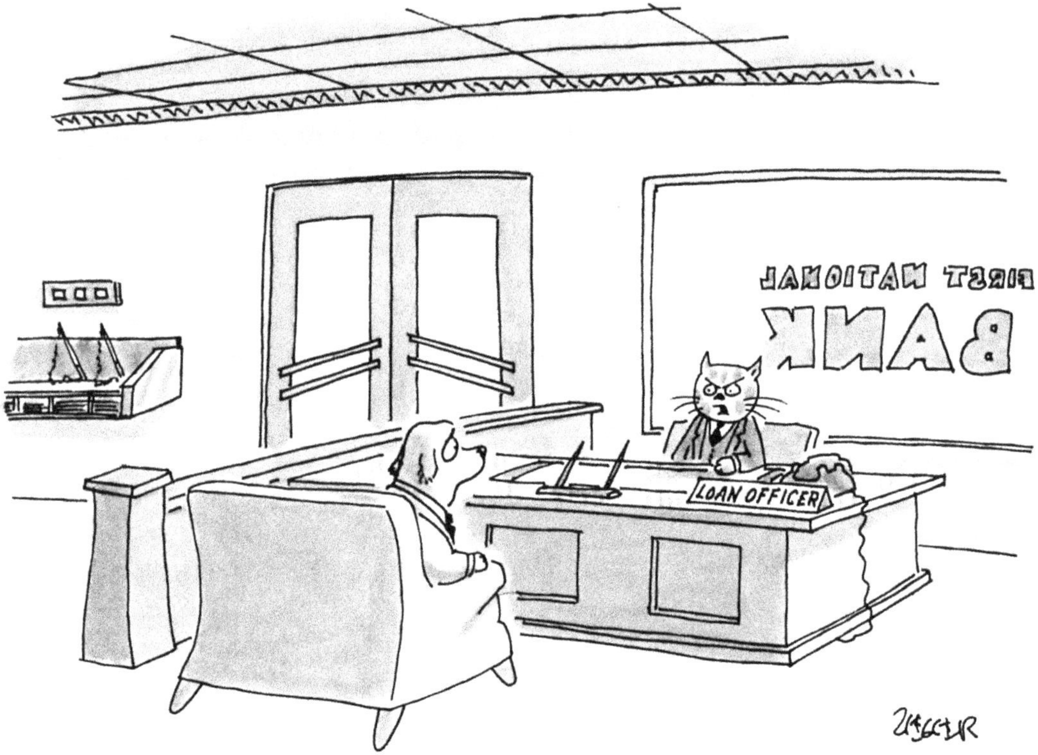
FIRST NATIONAL
BANK
LOAN OFFICER

"Beg."

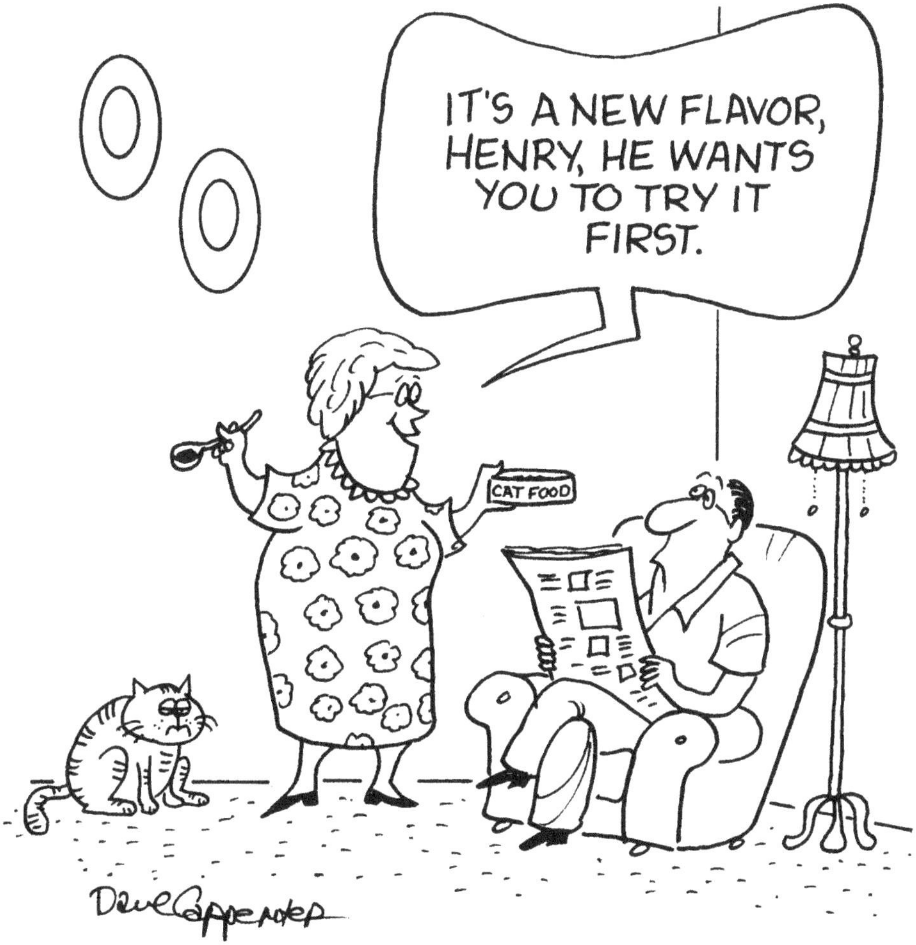
IT'S A NEW FLAVOR, HENRY, HE WANTS YOU TO TRY IT FIRST.
CAT FOOD

CAT RUN

GREGORY

(BEFORE)   (AFTER)

Dr. M. J. Pilkington
COSMETIC SURGEON

CALL 1-800-NEWFACE

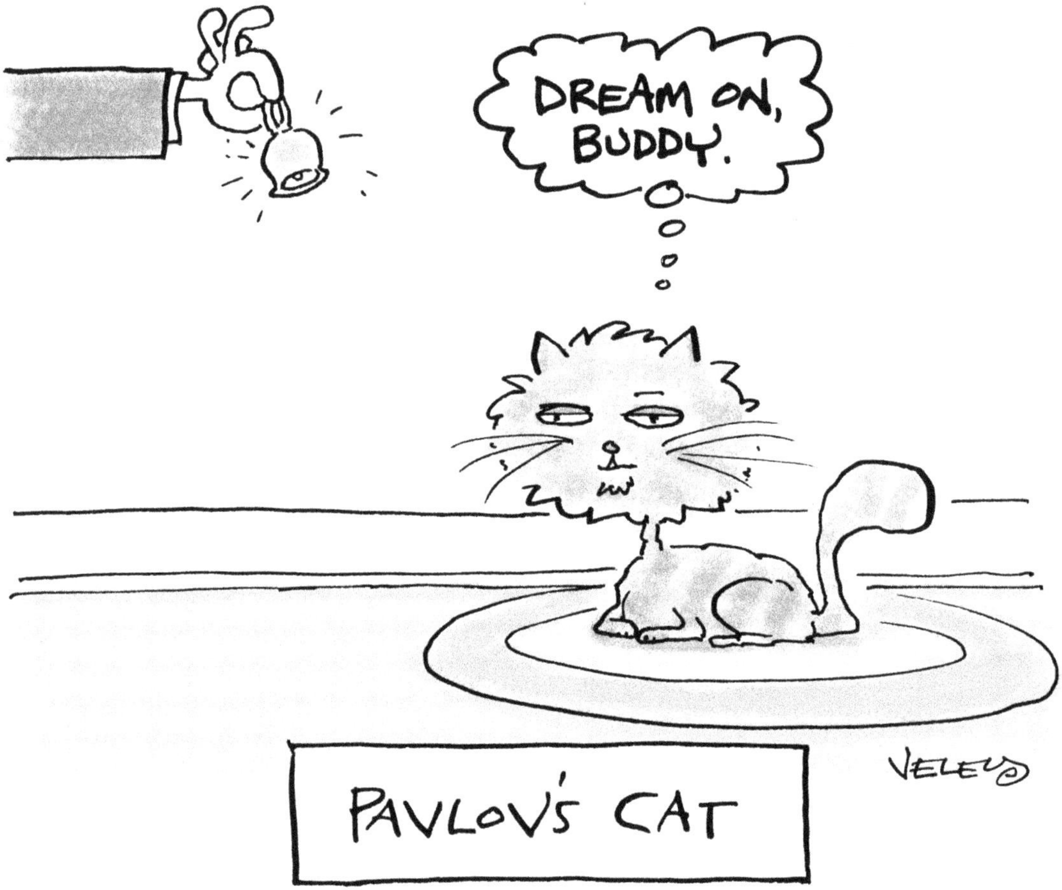
DREAM ON, BUDDY.
PAVLOV'S CAT
VELEZ

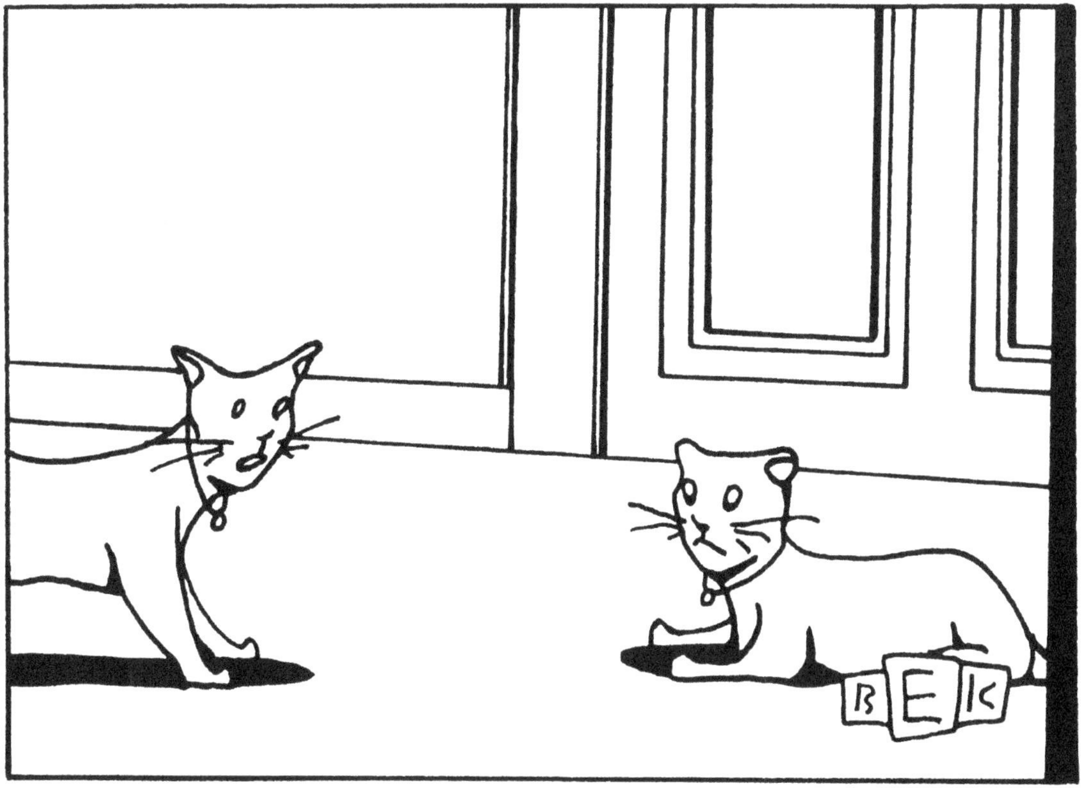
B
E
K

"People are O.K., but I prefer little pieces of string."

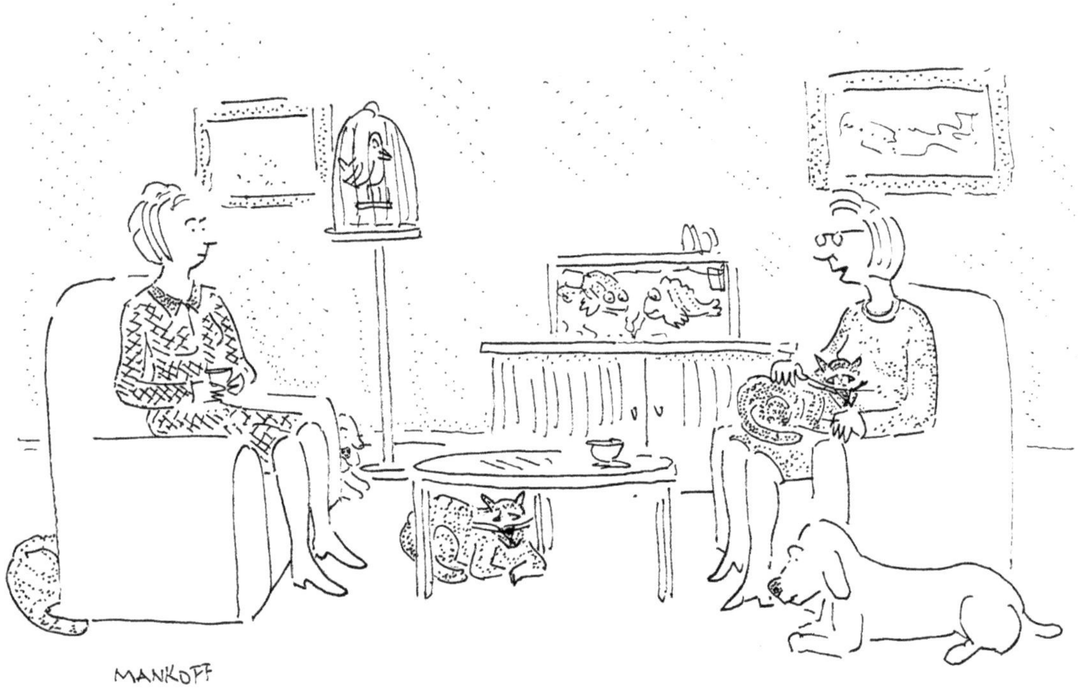
MANKOFF

"Look, children are just pathetic substitutes for people who can't have pets."

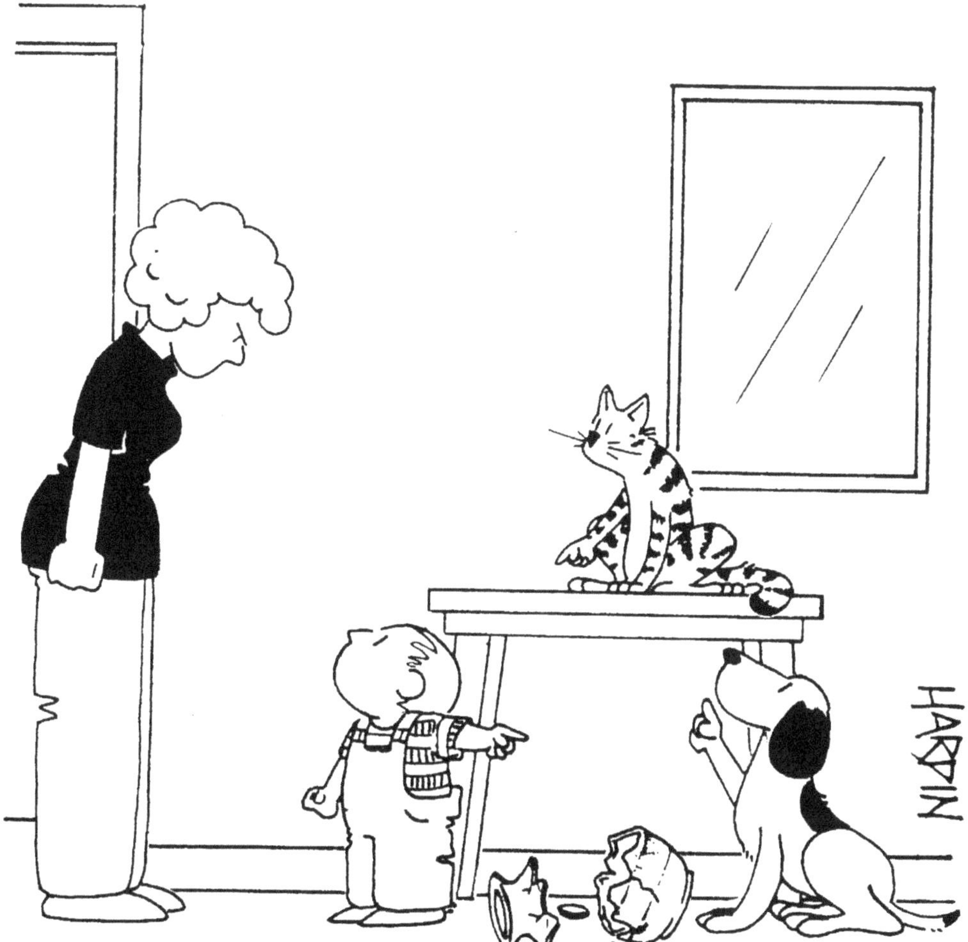
HARDIN

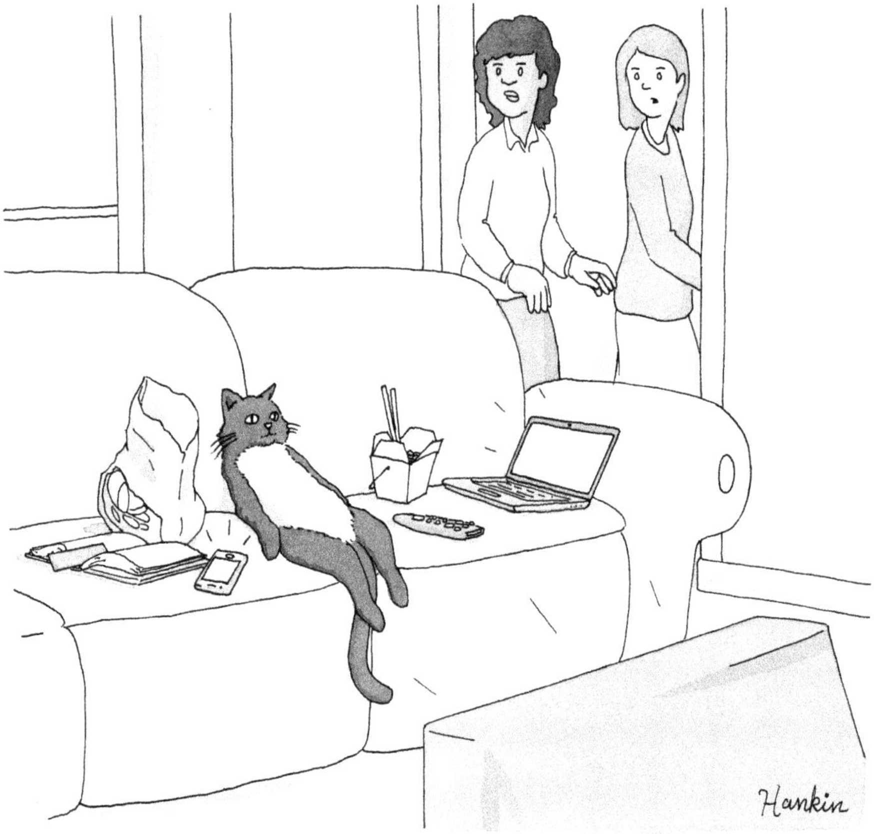
Hankin

"He's an indoor cat."

CAT KUNG FU

SO — THE DIET-COLA CAP RETURNS TO CHALLENGE THE MASTER!

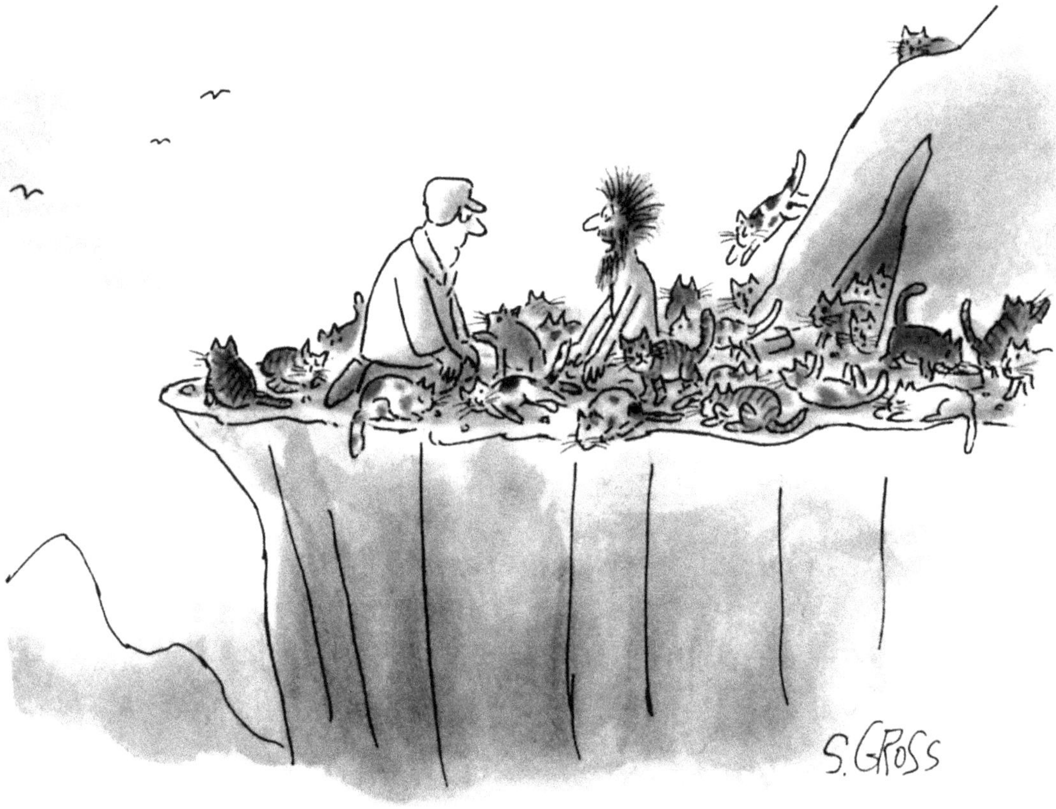
S. GROSS

"The meaning of life is cats."

"Can I call you back? I'm with a piece of string."

"I was a dog in a previous life, but I came back as a god."

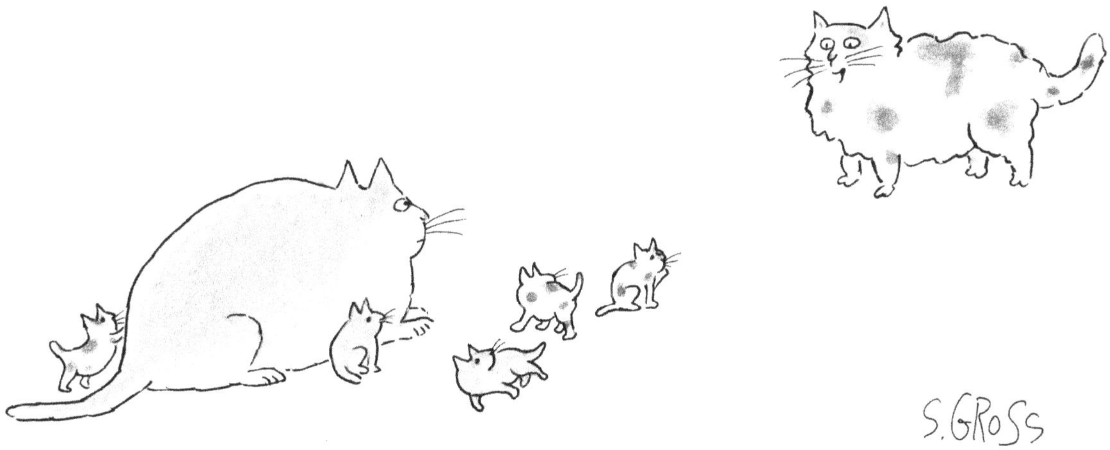
S.GROSS

*"Can I borrow those kittens for an hour?
I want to freak out the people who had me spayed."*

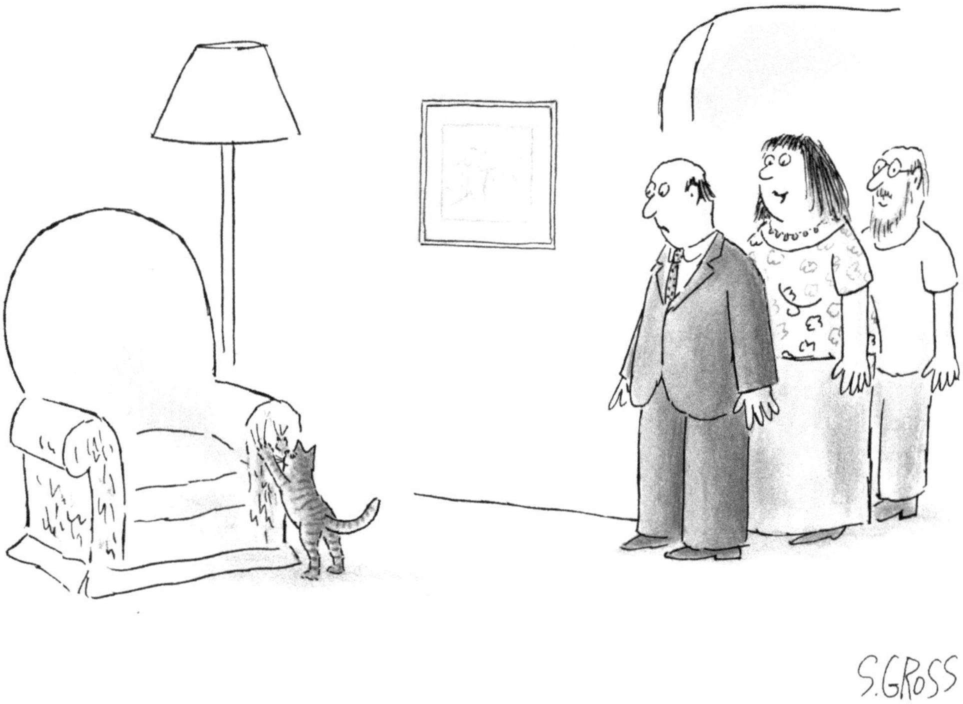
S.GROSS

"We believe that in a former life she was an editor."

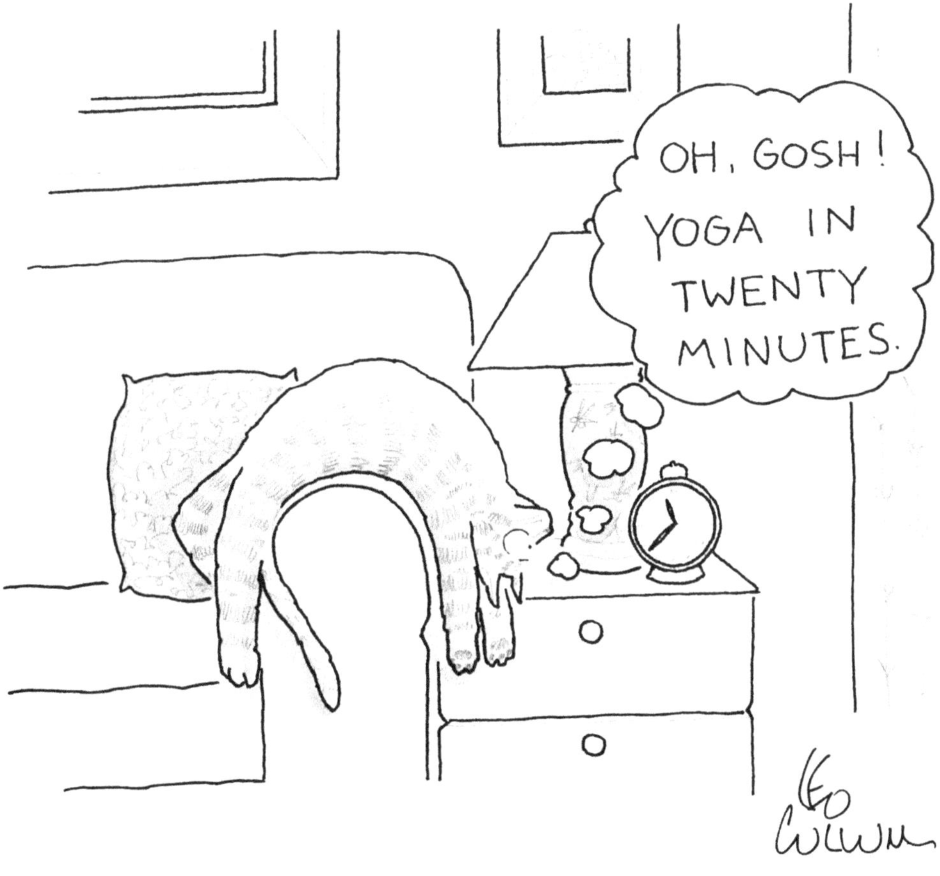
OH, GOSH! YOGA IN TWENTY MINUTES.

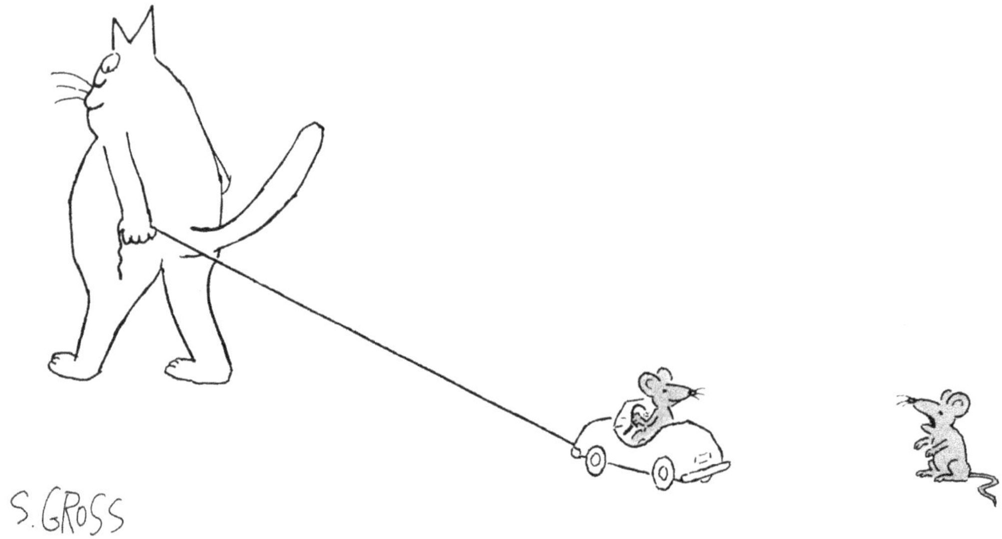
S. GROSS

"For God's sake, think! Why is he being so nice to you?"

C
c
d
D
E
e
g
b
a
h
f
A
B
ZIEGLER

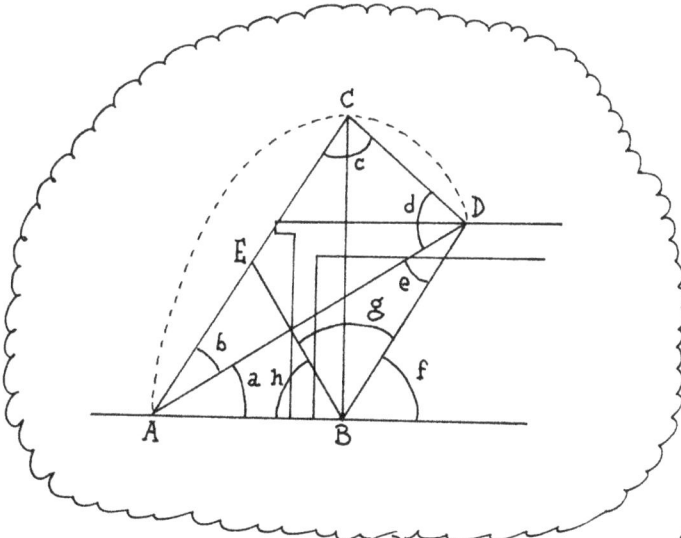

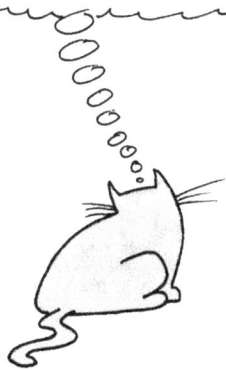

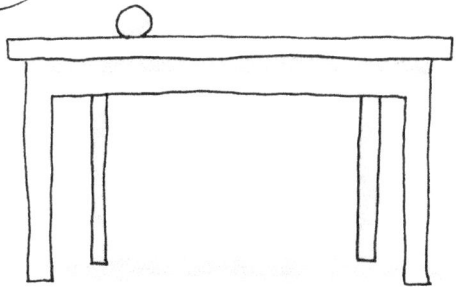

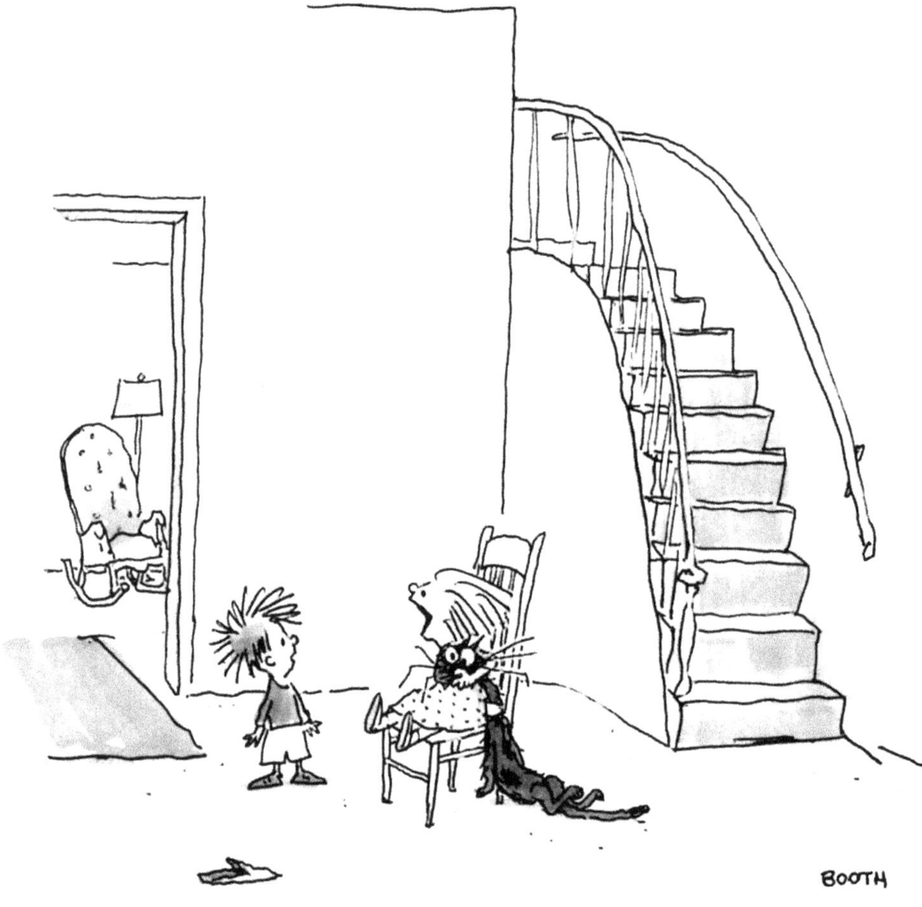
BOOTH

"All you really need in life is the love of a good cat."

"I have a couple of other projects I'm excited about."

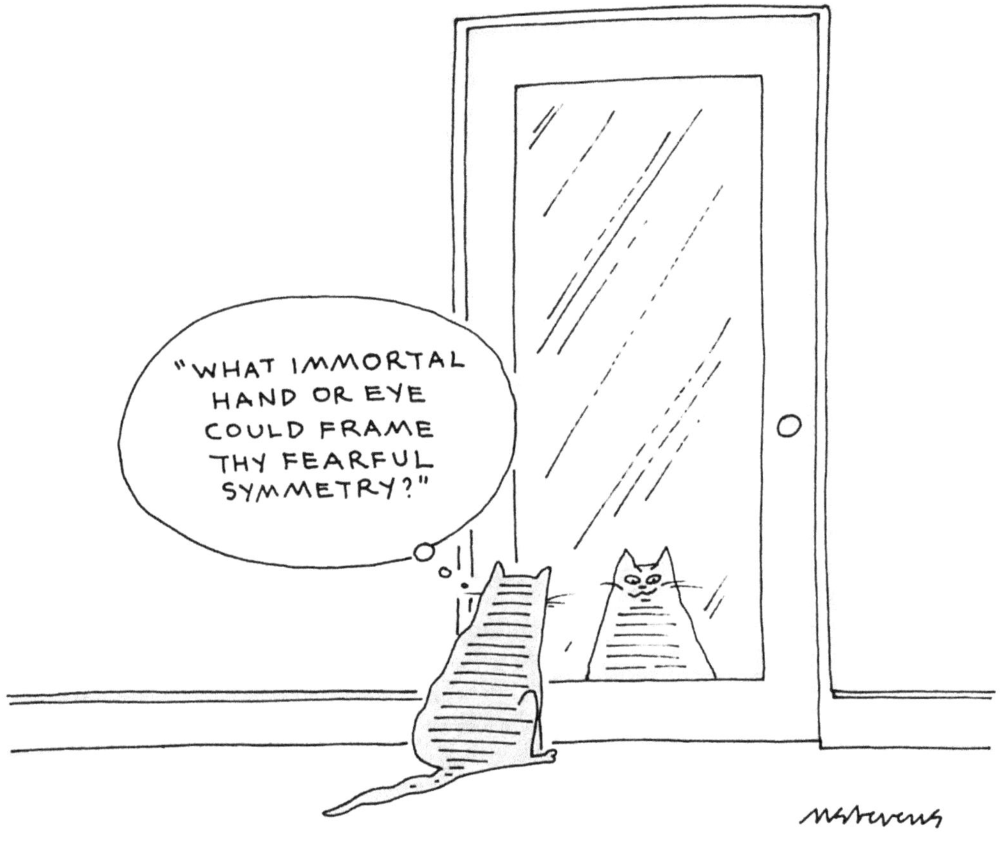
"WHAT IMMORTAL HAND OR EYE COULD FRAME THY FEARFUL SYMMETRY?"
MStevens

"*Never, ever, think outside the box.*"

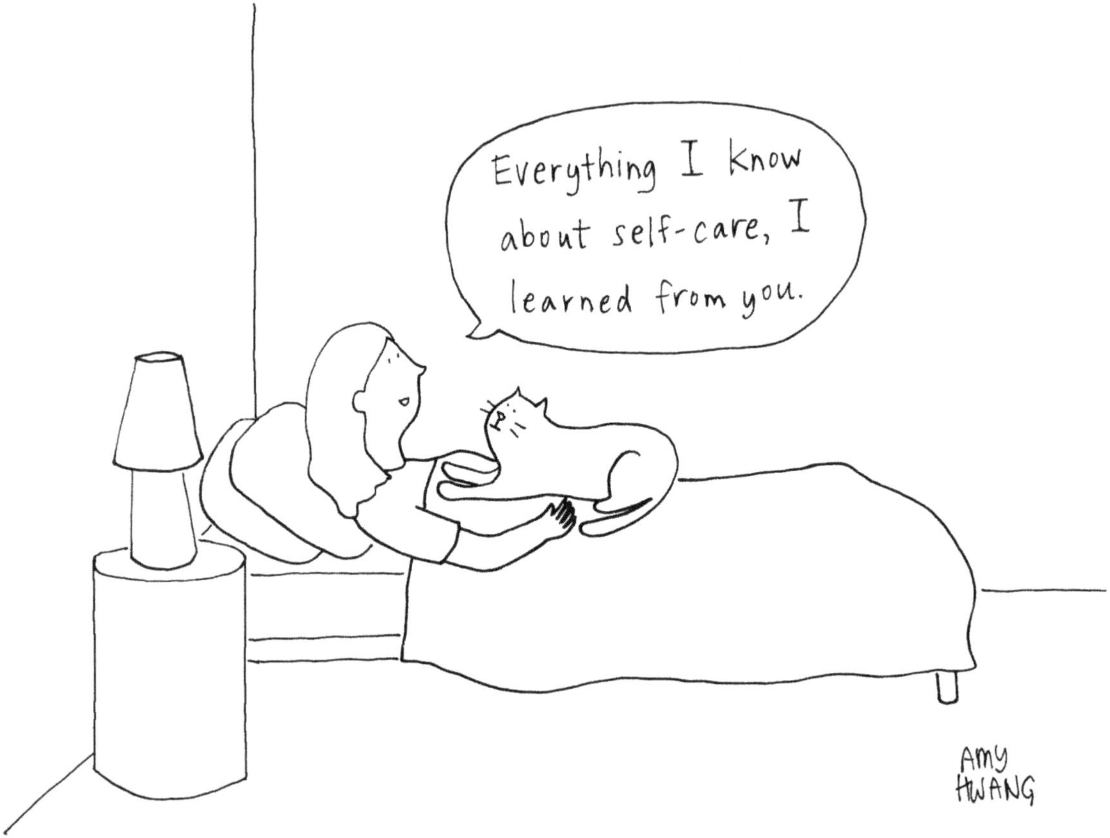
Everything I know about self-care, I learned from you.
AMY HWANG

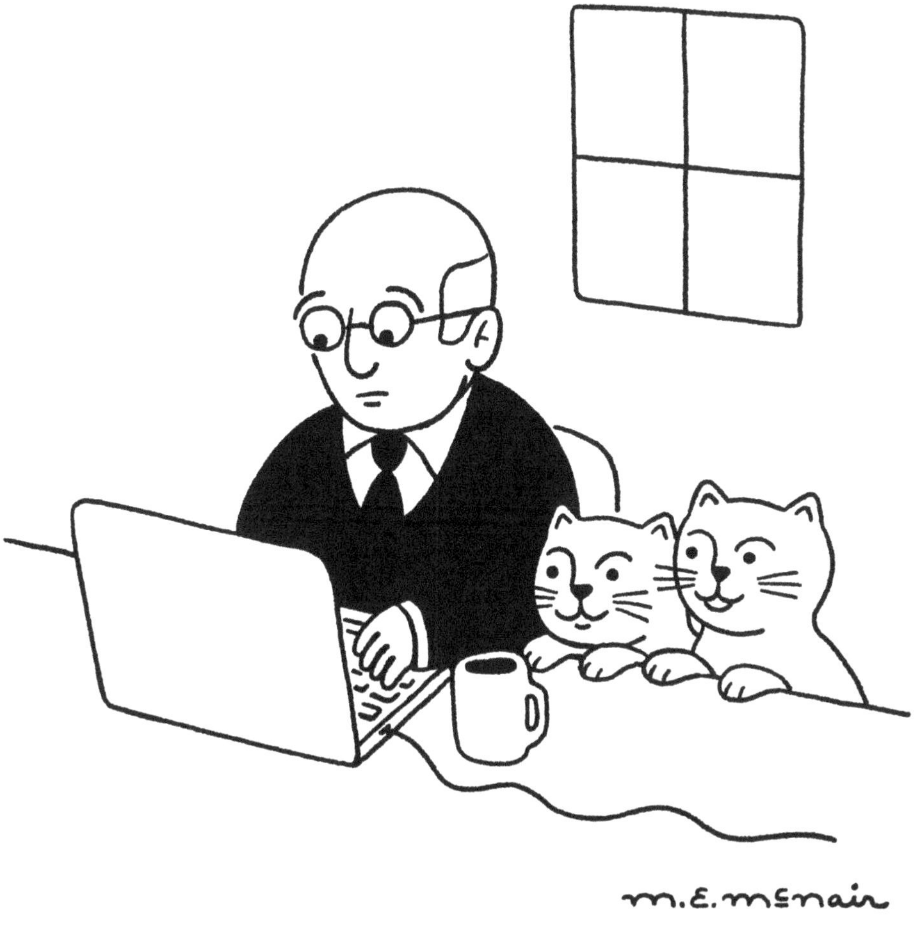
m.E. mcnair

"Remember, as soon as his boss joins the video conference, it's showtime."

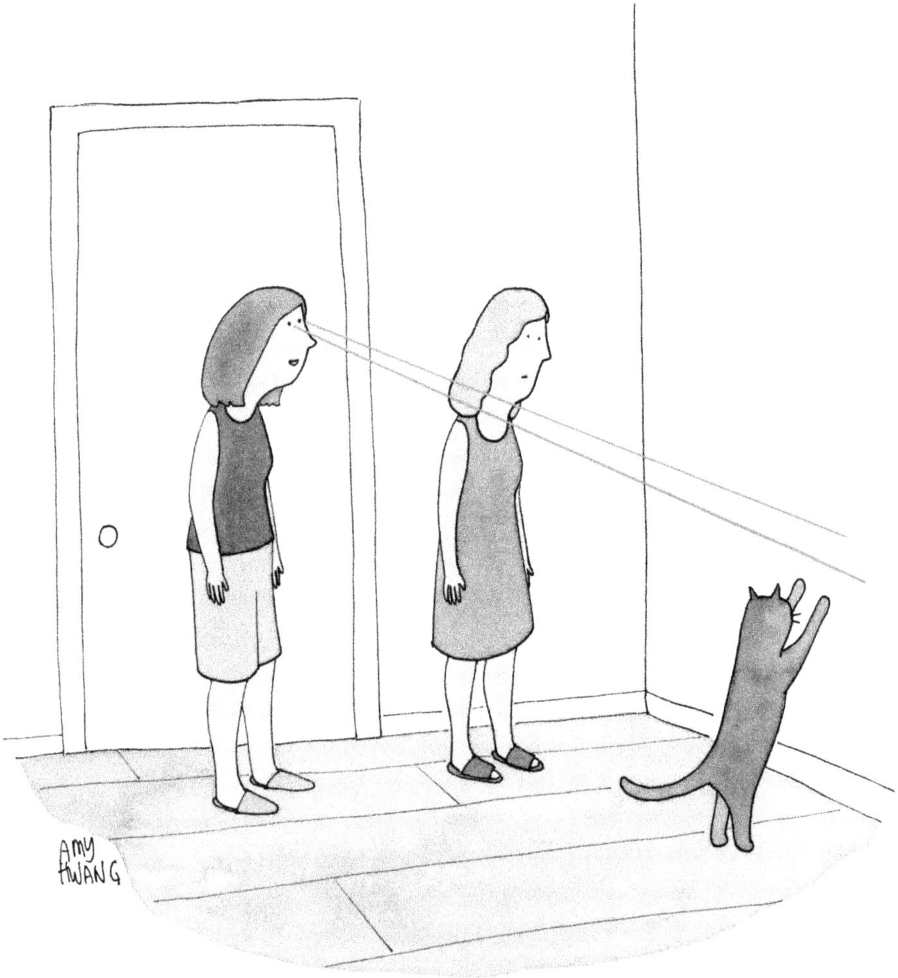
AMY HWANG

"My laser eye surgery was expensive but worth every penny."

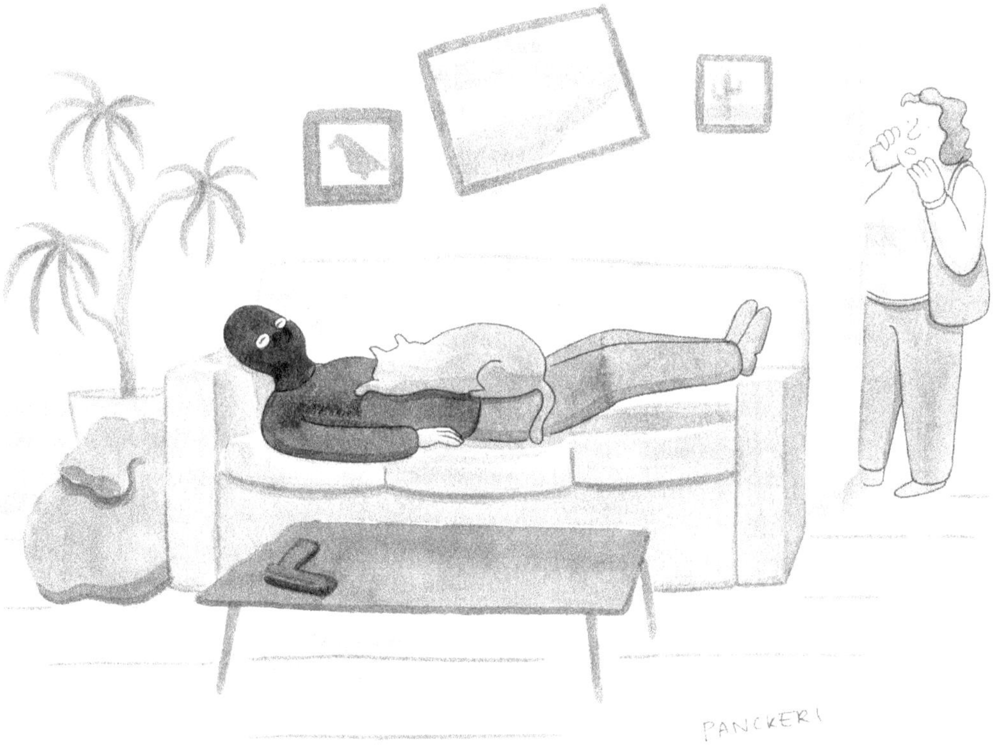
PANCKERI

"Please hurry—I don't know how long my cat can keep him subdued."

"*Stock options won't do it. I'll also need a ball of yarn.*"

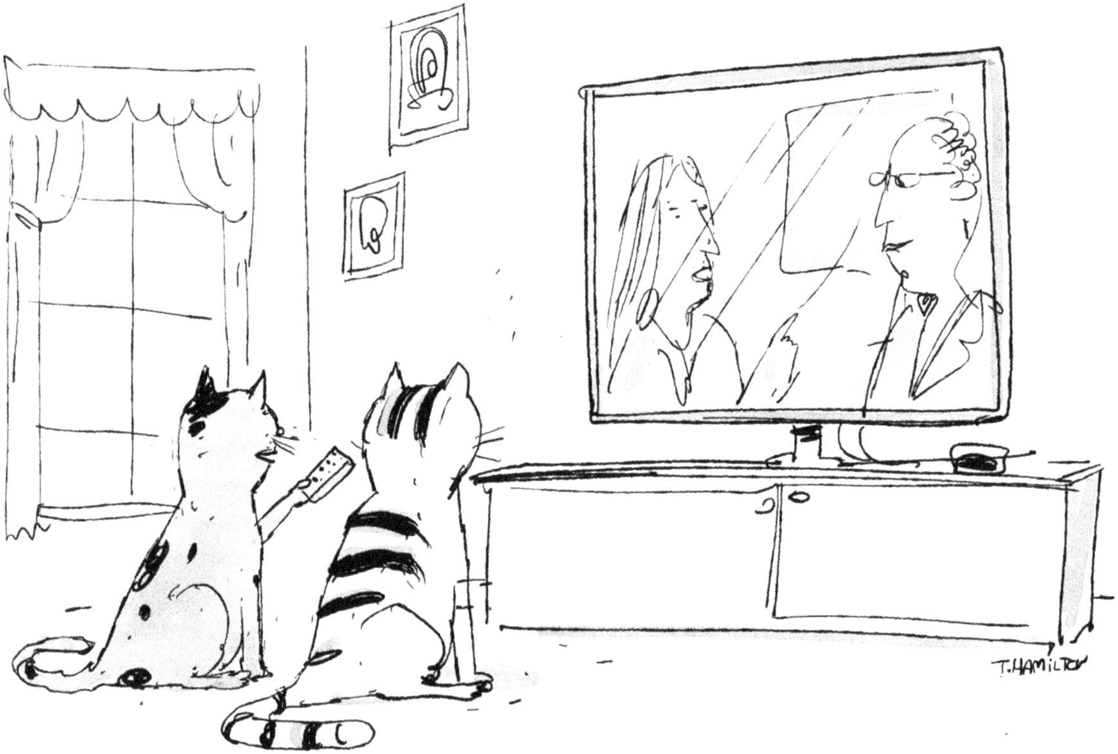
T. HAMILTON

"WIFI, Amazon, credit cards. Pretty much every password is named after me."

"I have a Bachelor's degree from Columbia, an MBA from Stanford, six years experience, and I'm a hell of a mouser."

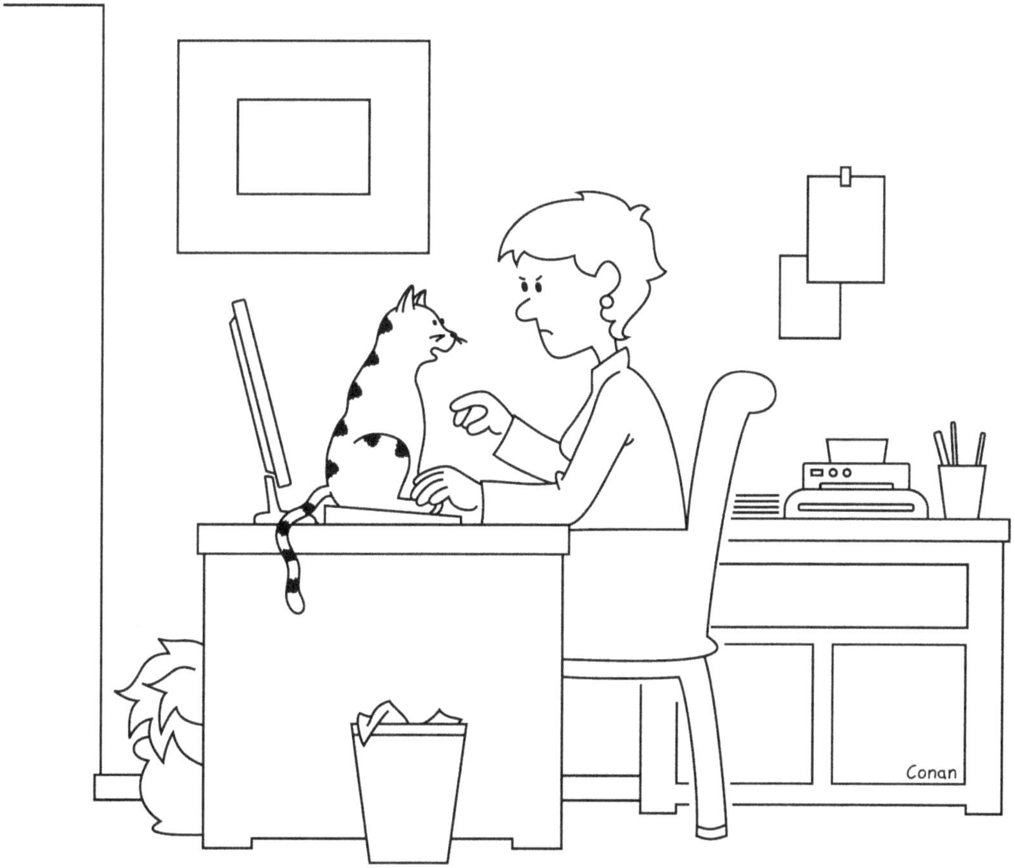
Conan

"Now you can stop watching those cute cat videos."

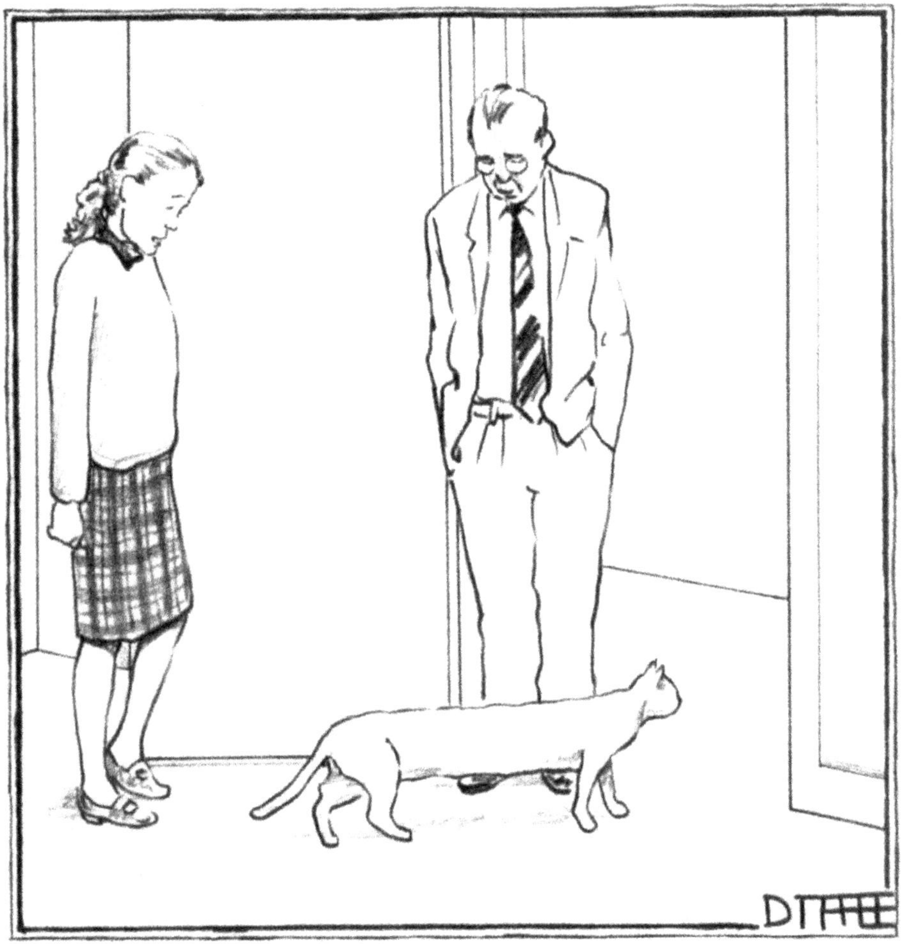
DIFFEE

"She's a weiner cat."

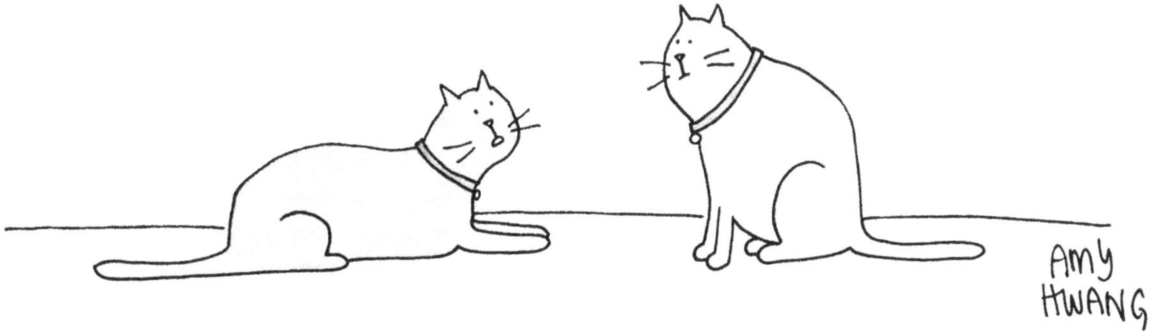
AMY
HWANG

"Is oversleeping a real thing?"

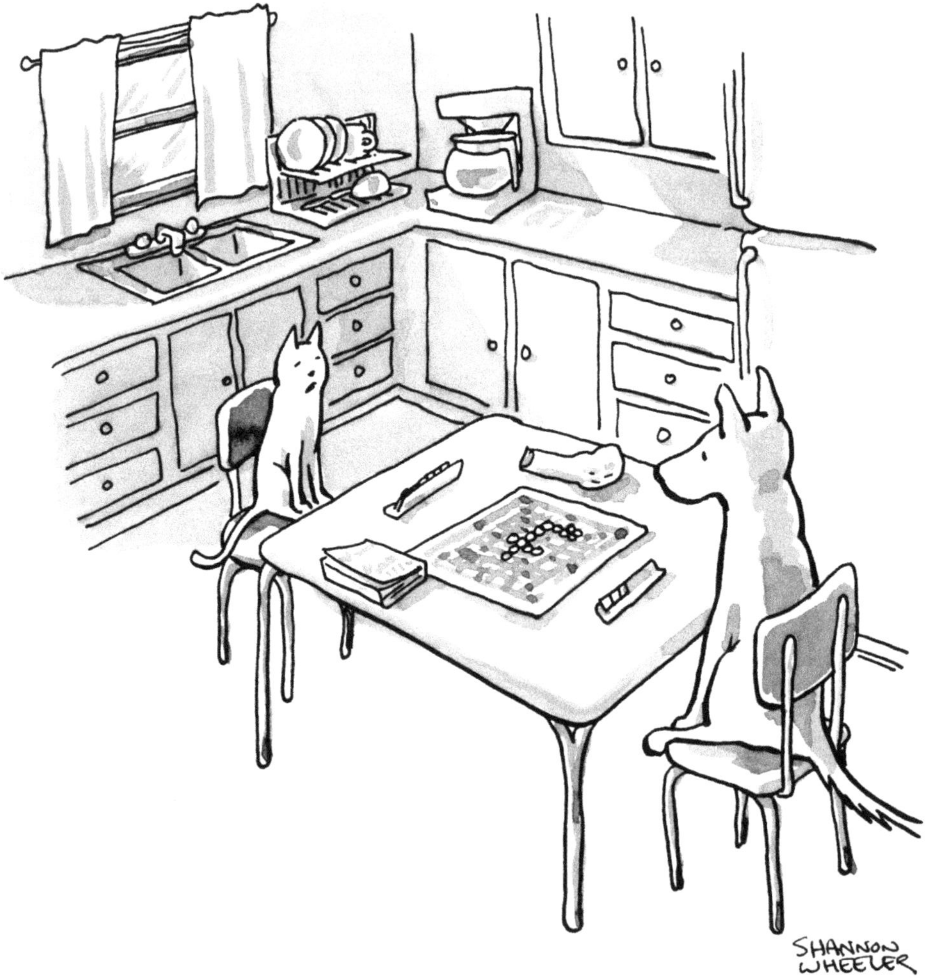
SHANNON
WHEELER

"'Grrr' is not a word."

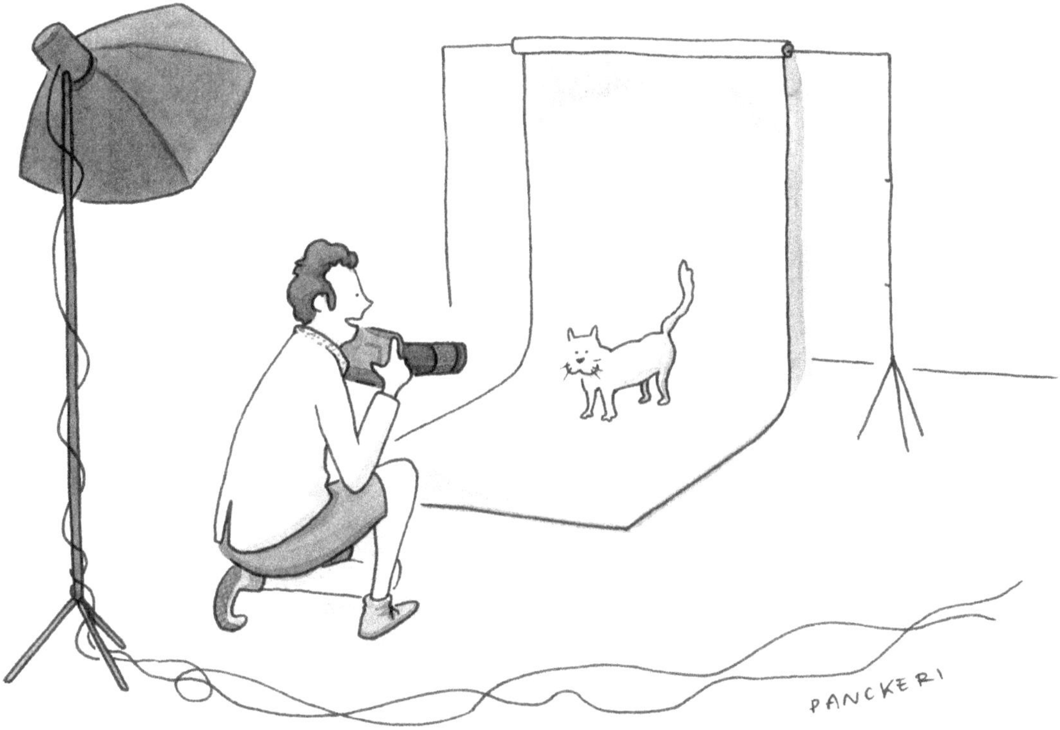
PANCKERI

"OK, give me something that says, it's two in the morning and you're feeling a little wild."

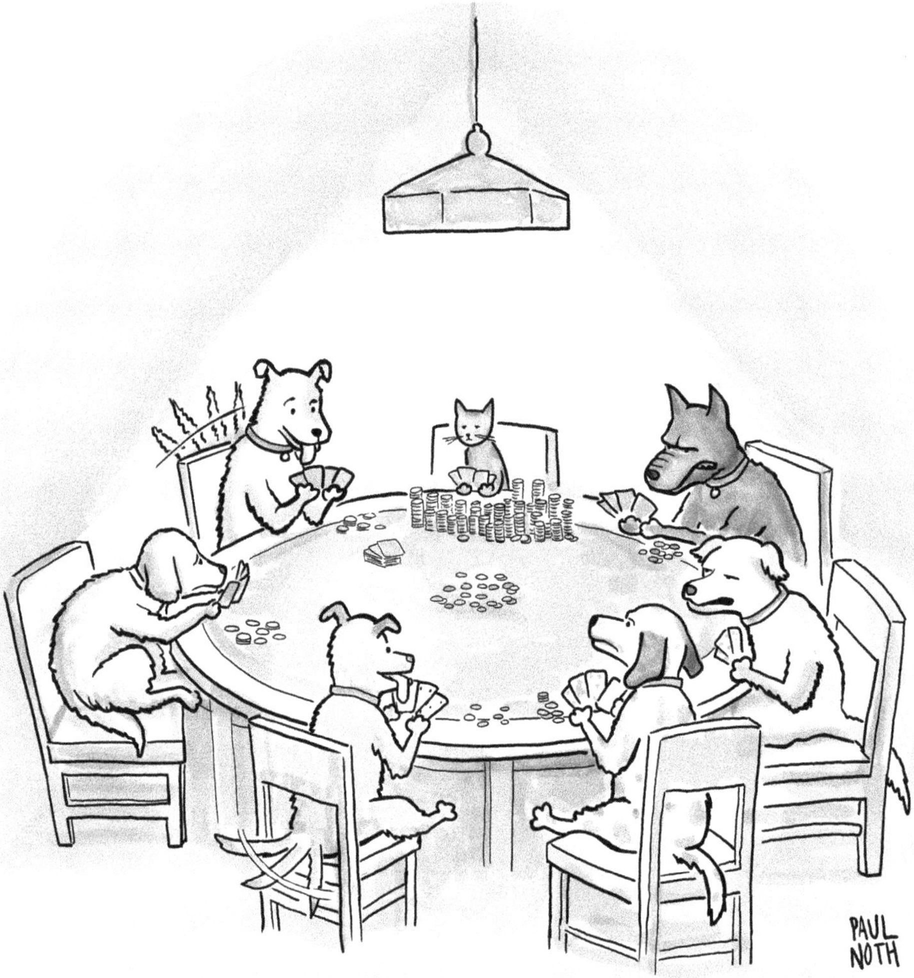
PAUL
NOTH

"If he has a tell, I haven't found it."

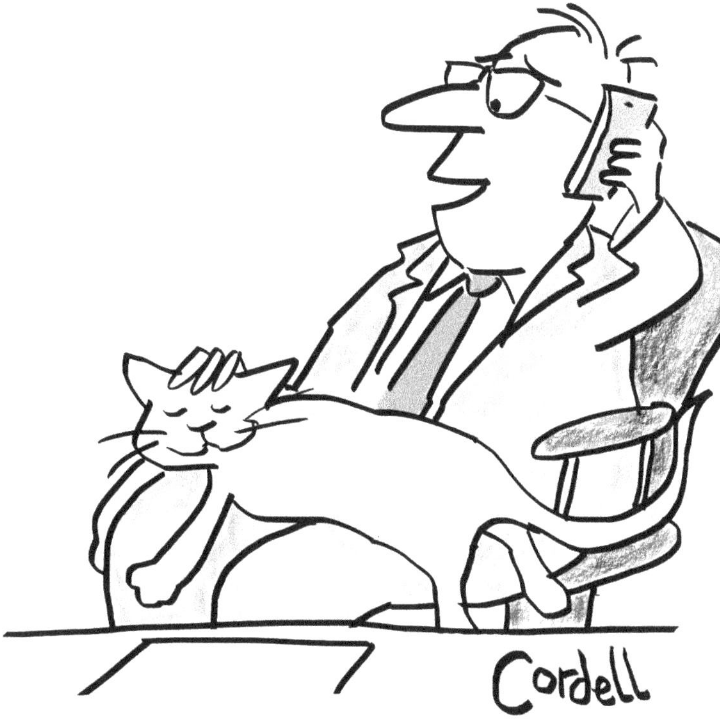
Cordell

"I'm sorry, but the position of Contentment Provider has been filled."

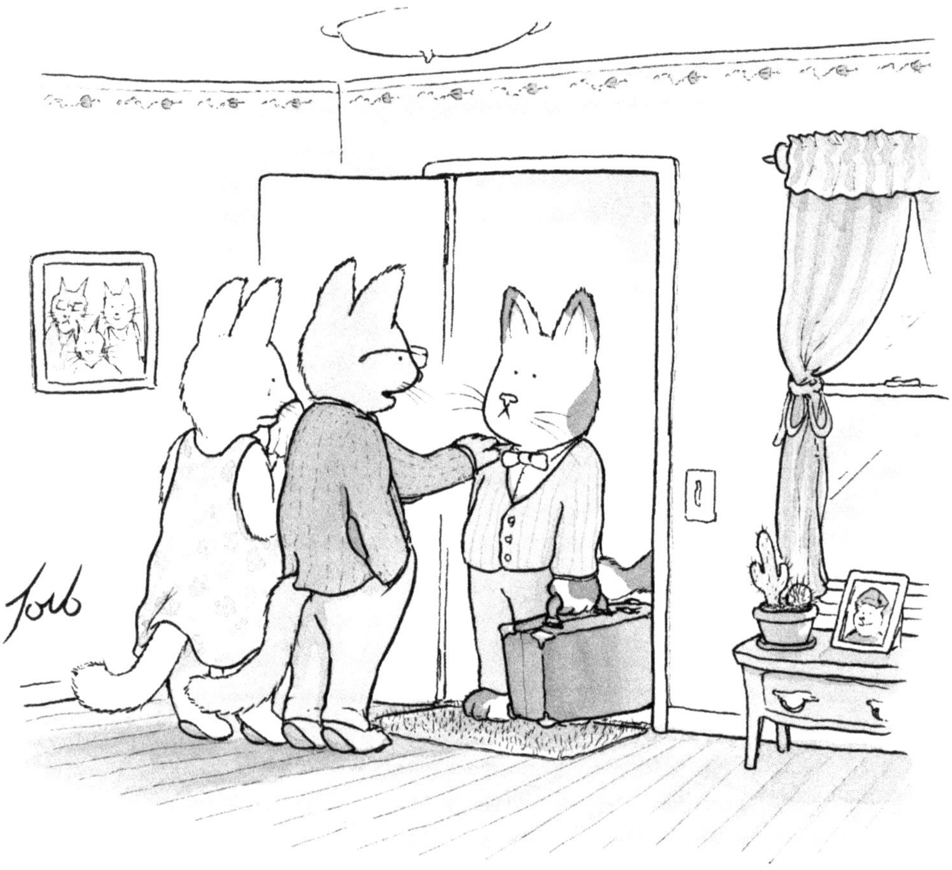
Toro

"Find a patch of sunlight, my boy. Find a patch of sunlight and bask in it."

"It's a lot easier than the mechanical bull."

Index of Artists

www.ingramcontent.com/pod-product-compliance
Lightning Source LLC
Chambersburg PA
CBHW062333150426
42813CB00078B/2742